What people are saying about *The 24 Hour*

"The best example of how students will r[...] their teachers! Not only did Mr. Kaiser's students reach and exceed his expectations, so did his school and community. The entire time I was reading it, I was thinking how we could try it here." —**Brett Fuller, 2014-2016 Wisconsin Health and Physical Education President**

"As a teacher, helping students learn and grow is my ultimate goal, and if you can do something that has a life-impacting affect on a large group of students, then you are doing something right. The 24 Hour Run Experience changes students' lives and helps them build character and persevere toward their goals. For that reason, I would recommend this book to my teacher-friends. I found the book inspirational and it got me thinking about how I could try to do something similar at my school." —**Tedd Markos, Physical Education Department Chair, Spark Academy, Lawrence, Massachusetts**

"24 Hour Run shows that finding motivation and passion in your life is the key to success. Through Fred's journey of trying to pull off this amazing event, he pushes his own limits and brings the entire community along with him. In recent history it seems that young people are given the option to quit at the first sign of adversity. It is refreshing to hear that there are still people like Fred who are willing to push young people to find their limits and learn they are much higher than they had originally thought." —**Clint Jones, 2 Time Olympian (Ski jumping), 2014 Olympic Head Coach (Ski Jumping), Team Director for USA Nordic Sport**

"Fred Kaiser's book should be read not only by teachers, but by every parent who has a young child entering the formative middle school years. His program offers a unique opportunity for students to learn the benefits of setting and achieving personal goals, working as part of a team, abiding by the rules, and accomplishing something they never thought was possible. Participants develop positive habits that last a lifetime, and parents can receive the much sought after bonding experience with their child. In this age of increasing dependence on electronic learning and overly protective parenting, it is refreshing to see the passion of teaching played out by Fred and his staff." —**William T. Jebb, Business Entrepreneur, former U.S. Navy UDT/SEAL Officer**

"Education is not the filling of a Pail, but the lighting of a Fire." This quote by Yeats captures the essence of the stories and experiences from the 24-Hour Run at Lundahl School. Fred Kaiser's sense of passion has created a ripple effect of life changing experiences for the students, the staff, and their community. There is something of value in this book for everyone." —**Dan Creely Jr., TEAM Conference, Professor Emeritus, Northeastern Illinois University**

"This inspiring book is a must read for physical educators ready to take their message out of the classroom and into the community. Fred's enthusiasm for his work is obvious as he explains how this experience changes the lives of the staff and students, as well as parents who watch their children grow into young adults." —**Steve Palmiter, Adventure/Health/ Physical Education Teacher, Robert M. LaFollette H.S., Madison, Wisconsin**

Frederick Kaiser

The

24

HOUR

RUN

EXPERIENCE

Building Characteristics of Success
One Step at a Time

wnb
WOODNBARNES
open books • open minds

Published by:

Wood N Barnes Publishing
2309 N. Willow, Suite A
Bethany, Oklahoma 73008
800-678-0621
woodnbarnes.com

Photographs by Frederick Kaiser and Sarah Johnston

Original cover design by Michael Neamand

Interior designed by Ramona Cunningham

Printed in the United States of America

ISBN 978-1-939019-18-9

Contents

https://www.youtube.com/watch?v=zz1PaXFo8lI
(24 Hour Run – video by Dist. 47)

https://www.youtube.com/watch?v=mYpimmITp9g
(24 Hour Run – video by Brandon, former student)

https://www.youtube.com/watch?v=uWseWr0rxC4
(Fitness Marathon – video by Fred Kaiser)

■ Preface

If something happened in your life that positively impacted thousands of students and families, would you share the information? That's what teachers do. We share for the benefit of our students to provide the best opportunity possible for everyone. The 24 Hour Challenge Run has changed how I teach, increased the attitude and motivation of my students, and received unbelievable support from the parents. It has had a positive impact on the overall climate of the school since its beginning in 1999.

For most of my career I have shared my lessons, teaching style, theories, and techniques, but I have also learned so much from others who shared with me. This book is intended to be a guide to educators, teachers to superintendents, for what's possible in education. It's a motivational piece for parents and students about experiences that can be carried forward in life. This manuscript includes the experiences leading up to the 24 Hour Run, hour by hour observations and reflections, and how the event is completed, along with inspirational quotes that tell the story.

I felt that I had to put this event and the experiences surrounding it down on paper for myself and for others. Writing a book was literally the last task I thought I would, or could, ever do but I took the risk and gave it my best. If nothing else, it has been great therapy for me to put my thoughts on paper and get them out of my head so that I can sleep at night.

The journey and the experiences have been powerful; they are both joyful and heartbreaking, but also successful. The ripple effect of this will continue for a long time. I hope this book inspires teachers and individuals to achieve something greater than they thought possible. First, to create an understanding of students' potential and the need to challenge them. Second, how success at something difficult can be a rewarding motivation to achieve more. Success is a powerful motivator. Learning how to be successful and putting it into practice repeatedly can be life changing.

Why We Teach

Why do teachers teach? It is our passion; it is what we love to do. For many, we spend much of our time outside the classroom thinking of ways to better our lessons, considering how to reach certain students, and looking for inspiration to bring to our students. Impacting the lives of others is a very pure, fulfilling experience. It comprises who we are, our skills and knowledge, our passion, and our ability to convey our message to positively change others' lives. That is a powerful responsibility. Making a difference can come from a small, seemingly insignificant, moment to the grand plan of a lesson. When teachers have students return for visits, or when they see them in the community years later, the question is, "Do you remember me?" Of course we do—well most of the time at least. Some more than others. Some have grown into barely recognizable adult versions of their youth, but teachers almost always remember something about their former students. The same holds true for our students. They will almost always remember something about us. The question is, what do they remember?

After ten years of teaching and coaching, I thought I was doing well as a teacher. My classes were motivating, I had great units and lessons, I demonstrated everything I taught, and kids were engaged and learning. I thought I was pushing the boundaries of what I could do with my students. Then I saw something that shook me to the core and let me know that I had only scratched the surface. I had no idea the journey I was about to take was going to change my life and the lives of so many others.

GIANNA

I just graduated college. It has been 8 years since my last 24 Hour Run. I can honestly say it's my favorite school memory. It single-handedly taught me determination and perseverance. I never underestimate my strength. I owe my drive, passion, and perseverance to the 24 Hour Challenge Run and the teachers and parents who gave me this opportunity. I am forever thankful.

Inspiration

We judge ourselves by our intentions and others by their (actions) behavior. —**Stephen Covey**

Quotes are interesting. They are simple, to the point, and can succinctly convey an entire story. When I was younger, quotes didn't impress me as much as now. At this point in my life, quotes have a certain simplistic clarity to them and can be used as guideposts. Many times we find inspiration in these quotes or from the person telling the story. The above quote was one of the first ones that got to my core. It was so observant and correct. It helped motivate me to act on my ideas instead of thinking about them. Many people talk about their intentions but never following through; I wanted to follow through first. This tends to pull a lot more weight with people. I had to take more risks because I knew the end results, if achieved, would be worth the effort.

My biggest opportunity to take a risk came from an idea I heard in a presentation. Every year I attend the state convention for physical education. Illinois is fortunate to hold the largest state convention of its kind. This allows teachers to share ideas with others. As always, there was an abundance of "cool," interesting, new techniques and equipment we could get right from the source. I found myself, over the years, following several people I thought had really interesting presentations.

People like Dan Creely, Bill Quinn, and Carl Rohnke, who were all adventure and team-building legends in the profession I enjoyed. For nearly ten years, I also followed a gentleman named Tony Calabrese. I was engrossed with his presentation style and the challenging and fun activities he showed. I always brought back bits of information and activities for my class. What was missing for me was a long-term goal for my students, something that would put into practice what I taught all year. I needed something I could hang my hat on as a backbone or philosophy of my teaching. Anyone that knows Tony, knows he is a bit of an adrenalin junkie when it comes to adventure and testing limits. It was impressive to hear stories about how he had challenged himself or information on other people from around the world that he talked about or personally knew. To know that people did these activities was always motivating, but it was also demoralizing for me to know I had sat idle way too long. It was when he started talking about an event he did with his students that I knew I had found what I was looking for.

The challenge was simple—run in teams in one mile rotations, much like a relay, for 24 hours on the school track. At the time, this was the senior final exam for his high school physical education class. It was either do a 24 hour run or participate in a triathlon. It was a test of all they learned in his class, and it wasn't going to be easy. Participants had to prepare and support each other. That's what Tony does best with his kids, and they don't even realize it until later. By exam time, they are ready and willing. The difference with Tony Calabrese is that he made his students want to perform on their own intrinsic motivation. Such ability is powerful to instill in others. As teachers that is what we aim for with our students. We want them to achieve because they want to, not because they have to. Tony Calabrese went into the details of his event, and I could not take notes fast enough.

Susie Johannesen, a physical education teacher and colleague, was with me at the presentation, and she felt the same way. We knew we had to do this! If we made some alterations to the setup and made it voluntary instead of mandatory, could we do this? Would kids sign up? After all, we had good students that seemed to enjoy class, we knew they could be motivated for specific challenges, and we had the space. After giving it thought, I felt this was a doable project. Before I made a commitment, I wanted to call Tony to see what he thought.

Now Mr. Calabrese is probably one of the most positive and enthusiastic people I know, so I wasn't prepared for his response: "Oh, I don't know. Why don't you start with something a little smaller?" For a moment I didn't know what to say. Here was the guy I had followed for ten years, and he didn't have confidence in me or maybe the age group. One constant every successful person experiences in his/her life or career is rejection. At some point, someone tells that person "No" or "You can't …." This becomes a make or break moment. Does the person follow that response, let go of the dream, and go on about life, or does s/he stand strong to their conviction and prove others wrong. I was determined to do this project. Tony didn't say "no" but it cut like it. It was that little comment that lit a fire in me. I was even more convinced that I knew my students and my abilities, and that our school could pull this off. When the conversation ended, I had his blessing and support; however, I felt that he knew the event might not be successful. After six years of Mr. Calabrese presenting this relay, no one had tried it but me! Getting Mr. Calabrese on my side was the easy part; everyone else was going to take some work.

"Why would anyone want to run every couple hours and do that all night?" was the response Susie and I got from our principal, Rick Carlstedt. It wasn't that he did not support us, he just did not know why people would want to participate in such a demanding program.

After some discussion, he agreed, "Okay, fine. But I want some more information before you move forward with this, and see if any kids are interested in the event first."

He was right on one point: **Why?** We presented **what** and **how** instead. We approached our principal the wrong way. We definitely had to approach the students differently to get them interested. It all come down to **why** we were doing it, not **what** we were doing. Just like anyone else, principal Rick Carlstedt liked to receive information in a certain order. We had to present it in the way that was easiest for him to digest, not necessarily the way we wanted to propose the project. After some retooling and refining of details, the plan was to have all the information so he couldn't say no. It worked! Now, could we get the students to buy into it, follow through, and complete the event?

 LINDSAY

Every year my parents have given me reasons why I shouldn't do it but I did it anyway, and, best of all, I've never walked just to prove them wrong.

Motivating Others

If you want something you've never had, then you have to do something you've never done. —**Unknown**

Set the tone right off the bat. Motivation starts at the beginning; light a fire in students that will burn throughout the training and the event. The trick is to get them to want to do something. "Leadership is the art of getting someone else to do something you want done because he wants to do it." —Dwight D. Eisenhower. That is a great quote, but like it says, there is an art to doing this, and we didn't need to inspire just one person but several hundred middle-school students.

A meeting was set for after school; any students interested in doing the 24 Hour Run could attend and receive information about the program. One would have thought it was an all school assembly from the turnout. Hundreds of excited and curious 6th, 7th, and 8th graders filed into the gym ready to get the information. With everyone sitting on the gym floor, it might be tough to get the group to maintain focus, listen without talking, and not use their phones. But for the next 30

minutes; not a sound from anyone. Why? It's not allowed. Students who do not comply will be told to leave and will not be welcomed to participate in the event. Students knew that I was serious about this, firm with the requirements, and that this activity was for them. If we are not strict, the integrity of the program will be lost. I've never had to kick anyone out!

It all starts with **why** and the Golden Circle (see Figure 1). I heard a presentation on the Internet on TED.com by Simon Sinek on "How great leaders inspire action." For me it made sense. It clarified why some teachers, coaches, business leaders, and others were so successful. According to Simon Sinek, people know what they do, how they do it, but not always why (purpose, cause, belief) they do it. We normally work and communicate from the outside in, but the best companies and leaders (teachers) work from the inside out. They don't want others to buy what they do, they want them to buy **why** they do it. The goal is to get others to buy into believing what you believe.*

Biology: Looking at a cross section of the brain from the top down is similar to the Golden Circle.

- The outer, newest brain is responsible for rational, analytical thought and language.
- The middle two sections make up the limbic sections responsible for all of our feelings (trust, loyalty, responsibility for all human behavior and all decision-making).

When one communicates from the outside in, people may understand facts and figures, but it doesn't drive human behavior. When we communicate from the inside out, we talk directly to the part of the brain that controls behavior then allows people to rationalize the tangible aspects. This is known as a "gut decision" as opposed to the reverse where people say "it doesn't feel right." Loyalty comes from the **why**.

If I hire people just because they can do a job, they will work for money. If I hire people who believe what I believe, they will shed their own blood, sweat, and tears. Are you driven by a cause or belief or by the paycheck? Again, people don't buy **what** you do, they buy **why** you do it. What you do proves what you believe.** Teaching is the same when it comes to motivating kids, and has the same results at any age.

---

* ** Simon Sinek – "How great leaders inspire action." www.StartWithWhy.com

Leaders hold a position of power or authority, but those who lead inspire us. We follow people who lead not because we have to, but because we want to, and not for them but for ourselves.* If we can do this in the classroom, it can be extremely powerful and is the basis for how the 24 Hour Run is presented to the students.

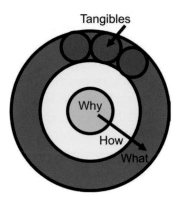

Figure 1: The Golden Circle**

Why: Everyone wants to and can achieve powerful accomplishments. We give examples of achievement, especially ones against all odds. People like to be a part of something great and experience success by doing so. It's a chance to find that inner strength and prove what they can do.

How: The 24 Hour Run is the outlet or tool. It becomes the activity that allows us to prove to ourselves what we felt or hoped we could achieve.

What (Tangibles): The challenge is to run, one mile at a time, on a relay team for the entire 24 hours.

If we presented this the other way around, I'm confident we would not have the success and turnout that we have over the years. With hundreds of students volunteering to take part each year (33% - 48% of the school population), it's a formula that works.

We are the most efficient species on the planet when it comes to running. Of course we don't have the power of a horse or the speed of a cheetah but we do have a feature that allows us to run farther—we sweat. This basic ability enables us to keep the body and muscles cooler, allowing us to run farther. I want students to know they are capable of running farther than they think they can. Most teenagers have the physical capacity to jog ten miles without stopping. This is surprising to most of them because they dread the mile run in class. This is never given out as a challenge but as a statement. Over the years, students have tested this theory successfully, jogging ten miles on their own without walking or stopping.

---

* ** Simon Sinek – "How great leaders inspire action." www.StartWithWhy.com

Where's the proof? I can talk to students all day about what their bodies are capable of, but it can be hard for them to relate. I like telling stories of ordinary people doing extraordinary things or overcoming great obstacles. If the story is about someone around the student's age, then they can visualize their own potential and relate. Jack LaLanne, Rick and Dick Hoyt, Dean Karnazes, John Stephen Akhwari, Terry Fox, Kayla Montgomery, and Nick Vujicic are just some of the people who have great stories. We share stories about Native Americans and how they become recognized as warriors in their tribes. These are stories of physical prowess and integrity. If accomplished, the person was given honor as a leader and/or warrior in the tribe. When I talk about these stories, it isn't until the very last sentence that I let them know what makes the story powerful. It's the obstacle in that person's life that makes the story hit them emotionally and makes it fantastic. It's impressive enough to know what these people have done, but that last line hooks them and they'll remember the message. For many this is what will motivate them during the run and what they can learn to call on later in life.

What is it that makes some people successful and others not? When he talked about his 24 hour run, Mr. Calabrese asked everyone in the presentation what they considered to be the characteristics of success. Nobody really had a good answer, especially myself. But as he talked about what was needed to complete his event, the characteristics he listed made perfect sense. In fact these make sense in just about anything we do. The beauty of it? It's simplicity.

The Four Characteristics of Success

- **Willingness to Risk**: To risk is to give up what is secure, to try an unknown, unsure of the results.

- **Commitment to Integrity**: Be honest with yourself, others, and to the program or idea.

- **Determination to Stand**: Determine what you believe in or feel strongly about, and hold to that. For many, it is the right decision (stand) and you will not be deterred because of what others say.

- **Sense of Passion**: This is what will drive you through the difficult times when others will quit.

This is the underlying philosophy for everything I teach. It is the backbone to the programs I am interested in as an educator. Of course I want students to be active in class and increase their fitness levels, but that's not always the most important aspect of my lessons. I'm more interested in the whole student and the experiences they can get out of physical education. My hopes are that they will find something to impact their future in a positive way, and that they will be active as adults and take aspects of our programs to help them become successful. Taking part in this event will help catapult these goals into everyday life.

Application of these characteristics to the run is easy to identify and press into action. The **willingness to risk** is choosing to take part in the event. For many this is way outside their comfort zone. It could be the distances and the amount of times they have to run. For some this will be the first time they've ever slept over someplace else or camped in a tent. Any number of reasons may be a risk for someone. By stretching their experiences or limits beyond personal comfort zones, there is also the reality some may not be successful. Without risk people can become stagnant and not achieve anything more than what they are already doing. Our goal is to make them comfortable and teach them how to prepare for this experience so we can reduce the risk.

Commitment to integrity is the hardest characteristic to maintain, but probably the most gratifying if done correctly. Many of the students don't know the definition of integrity. The ability to be honest can be a real struggle for some. If we can teach them how and why this is

so important in a daily or weekly routine, then maybe we can guide them into seeing the benefits of their efforts. Anyone can cheat or take the easy way out, but no growth occurs and they never realize accomplishment. This also becomes part of our character. One has a greater sense of accomplishment knowing it's done right. This holds true when it comes to training and filling out the log sheets. These log sheet are used to keep track of and provide legitimacy to training. Are the students doing what they are supposed to do and being honest in fulfilling their requirements? If they are, they will feel the benefits in their running performance. Are they being honest to themselves and to us? The integrity of the event is also important. The only way the 24 Hour Run remains successful is to strive to maintain what it's designed to do: run when it's your turn, no walking, make sure the team is on task, participate in the program in the way it is intended, and work toward the set goals. If these basics can be followed, then the gratification of this challenge will be well worth the success achieved.

Many don't succeed because they are afraid of what others might think of them or their ideas. Conviction in our beliefs is vital. Holding to them when everyone else says something different is the goal—the **determination to stand** for beliefs. People, especially youngsters, will follow the herd and do what other people say in order to avoid judgement. They want to be accepted. Some middle-schoolers will have friends who do not want them to attend the 24 Hour Run meeting or to participate in the run. If the kids are determined to stand up to others and participate anyway, they will find they have taken a major step forward! Building confidence to make a decision on their own and follow through with it, without the needed support or approval of others, is the goal. Intrinsic motivation will go a long way and is ultimately a valuable goal students learn during the process and activities.

At 3:00 AM when your turn to run comes and you're tired, sore, cold, and have had little or no sleep, you have to find the passion to get up and run the mile. This is where a **sense of passion** will be essential. The interesting aspect about these characteristics is that they occur in the same order mentioned earlier. If we've been able to accomplish the first three characteristics, then all that's needed is the passion to see it through to the end. Knowing the possibilities instead of the limitations helps drive the passion to succeed at something great. The human body is an incredible machine both physically and mentally. When people understand its potential and the incredible feats it can achieve,

the drive to obtain those goals can become stronger. This goes back to **why** in the Golden Circle.

The 24 Hour Run is a tool to put these characteristics to the test. It's a great medium. When it comes to physical education, it also ties into so many other attributes that complement these characteristics and other learning experiences. Goals, leadership, selflessness, planning, organization, responsibility, communication, problem-solving, and self-analyzing/reflection are just a few. I want our students to walk away from this experience knowing they can apply these principles to other aspects of their lives, such as getting a job, working on a new project, setting goals. Over the years, students come back and tell me this experience has guided them and made them more successful in their schooling, their jobs, and life. I've heard families talk about how they now instill these characteristics into their kids and family. One parent related how they now use this as their business model and how well it adapts for them. These four characteristics also had to be used to get the 24 Hour Run off the ground.

> **Risk:** We were the first to try anything like this at the middle school level, and it was the first event we would organize. It was way outside our comfort zone, but we were confident.

> **Integrity:** We didn't sugarcoat anything to the administration, students, or parents, and we didn't change the event from the original idea.

Determination: When our principal felt no one would do this and doubted the program, we were determined to prove our idea.

Passion: It took seven months to prepare and an incredible amount of time and commitment from myself and others. If I stopped because it was too much time or work, it would show that I lacked passion. Passion is a must. It can and will surprise us. The difference it can make in students and life is clear.

Success breeds success. The result of running a successful program is that it becomes infectious, both in the program and beyond. It's a neat side effect. When people believe in themselves or the program, they are willing to do more because they have a taste of what they can accomplish. Motivation is now self perpetuating due to the success of the event. It's great to hear students say they've been training for the 24 Hour Run on their own, eight months before the event!

ANONYMOUS

I honestly thought I wouldn't be able to do this, seeing as I get called lazy, a pig, and even useless. I wanted to prove that everyone who doubted me was wrong. That I CAN do anything I want to do. I'm proud of myself for the first time.

Training & Log Sheets

Integrity has no need of rules. —**Albert Camus**

The community knows when it's 24 Hour Run season. With hundreds of students training on their own during the week, middle-schoolers are seen running in their subdivisions on a daily basis. The parents love this and the positive effect it has on the morale of the community. It is a positive, unexpected result of the run, and it's always satisfying to hear the parents talk about the program. Training for the event and the use of log sheets is key: preparation, documentation, integrity, motivation, responsibility, and goals are all integrated.

Training is simple. Each participant runs on his/her own twice during the week and logs the times. In class on a cardio day, the same students step up the distances each week. Runners start with a half-mile for the first week and work up to 2½ miles in six weeks. The physical training isn't that tough for most, but the mental aspect is just as much of the training. Physically they've got it in them, we just have to let them see it for themselves in small increments so they are mentally prepared for what's coming up. Part way through their training, we time all the students for the mile as part of their physical fitness testing. This is a chance to see how training makes a difference. One year, a student ran across the finish line and, upon getting his time, he began jumping and flailing his arms

and yelling, "YES, YES!" When I asked what was going on, he said, "This is the fastest mile time I've ever gotten." When students get their best mile-time ever or improve by several minutes, it is proof their training is paying off!

With everyone around us pushing themselves just a little more, we tend to push ourselves more. One of the great positives in preparing for the event is that on our cardio/fitness days no one walks. Many physical education programs with fitness days designated for jogging the track have no accountability or motivation to do just that, jog. In some schools, all they have to do is walk the track on those days. This is the fault of the teacher. Our job as instructors is to get kids moving, teach them why it's important, motivate them, and lead. Not doing this may be perpetuating the belief that physical education or fitness is unimportant. This behavior stems from lack of leadership. We work with all the students on why fitness is a benefit both mentally and physically, along with pacing, breathing, challenging themselves, and wearing proper shoes, etc., so that running doesn't become difficult, but easier. Having nearly half the school training helps those that are not in the program to keep up or try a little harder. This is a kind of passive, positive peer pressure that can be infectious.

As much as we would like to prepare the students for the challenge solely at school, curriculum and time are not in our favor. This means everyone has to run twice on their own at home, and we need to make sure they are following through. As minors, they are our responsibility. So, to help document this, the students must present their log sheet to us each week. Not only do they write their times for distances, we also have the parents sign off indicating the student did do this. Now we have the parents accountable, promising that they are keeping up with the minimum requirements. This is part of their integrity. Students need to be honest with themselves and with us. They need to get the training done even if it's cold, raining, or late in the evening or if they are out of town. I would be naive not to think that occasionally some parents may just sign the sheet or some of the training is not being done. The log, however, is something physical to show we've done our part as a school and department. Each week the students then run the required distance in class so we can see how they are progressing. If they walk during that time, they know it's elimination from the program. This is a way for us to keep tabs on everyone, and it helps to keep everyone honest and motivated.

My biggest ally and supporter, Susie Johannesen, was worried that first year that we were pushing the kids too hard in their training: "We've never challenged the kids this much, is this something they can really do and something we should expect from them?" We kept checking the "pulse" of the kids throughout the training to see if they were breaking down. Instead, they rose to the occasion and were performing beyond our expectations, not just because they could keep up with the training, but because of how many students were keeping up with the training.

It's all about motivation and responsibility when it comes to the log sheets. Not only can we see how the runner is keeping up with the training, but we can also gauge their motivation and responsibility. This is a great test for both, and it's simple: Turn in the log sheet in class every Monday. Of course absences are excused for the time they are gone, but it's due when they get back. We also understand that hiccups happen in life that prevent bringing in the log sheet on time. Split families are often problematic, late night responsibilities, or a student can just plain forget. So we worked out a grace period of Tuesday morning, but only the first ten minutes of school. This is allowed only three times out of the six weeks. If they don't turn in the log sheets by the deadline, they are eliminated from the program. This will test many, but it's a way to prove responsibility for something important. After all, they will be responsible for much more during the event, and if they can't turn in their log sheet on time, then I have concerns about their responsibilities at the event. It may sound harsh to eliminate students from the program for this. Shouldn't we let them have another chance so they can participate? It comes back to the **integrity** of the program. As soon as we let requirements slide, the program weakens, and the participants haven't learned anything. We do talk to the runners so they understand why this is important. Occasionally, we make an exception to the rules for special circumstances but not without something in return. In the past, parents have called to try and reinstate their child back into the program, and sometimes we make accommodations, but generally we stand strong on our own rules. Over the years, word has spread, and parents know that it's the child's responsibility and that

calling the teacher or principal is not what the program is about. Every year, students come back in 7th or 8th grade after being eliminated the previous year with comments like, "This year I'm going to make it!" They are more determined, perhaps because someone told them "No" the previous year. I tell the athletes nothing more than motivation is needed to turn in the log sheet filled out properly each Monday, and I can prove it: "If I were to give you a $100 bill every time you turned it in would you do it?" They all smile, most of them nodding their heads. "If it's important to you, you will find a way to make sure you get it in on time." This example makes the process and responsibility crystal clear. When we check in with students that didn't get their log sheets in on time, nearly all of them accept their responsibility and fate without discussion. By the time the run comes around, the ones that made it through the six weeks feel good about making it that far, and they are ready to run.

Students want to participate in the run, but what's the goal? Most athletes have a reason for attempting this event. For many it's because it is the largest social event of the year, and they enjoy the challenge. But what is driving them to make sure they make it through to the finish? What is their individual goal? We've added an area on their log sheet to help keep the students focused and allow them to see what they can accomplish. Goals like, "I want to make it the entire 24 hours" or "To make it without walking" are expected. Just like, "I want to stay up all night" has nothing to do with the run. We ask them to write down a personal challenge or the particular reason why they are doing the event. For most it's the amount of miles they would like to run or a time they would like to beat. For the 8th graders, it may be a desire to be a team leader and take on responsibility to help their team members if needed. Every so often we get those goals that tug at your emotions.

In any case, we let them know that just by writing down your goal and looking at it everyday, you have an 86% chance of achieving it. If you don't do this, you have a 30% chance of achieving the goal. This simple line on their goal sheet has gone a long way in keeping the runners focused and providing a purpose during the event.

ANONYMOUS

In 6th and 7th grade I had really bad anxiety during the run, and in 8th grade I made it my personal goal to be able to control my anxiety and be more independent. I really believe that I have achieved this goal and become a calmer, more decent person. The run has showed me how to be able to control my feelings and focus on having a good time.

Planning & Organization

Challenge the impossible! —**Unknown**

In the next 24 hours several hundred students will collectively run 5,000+ miles. They will eat and sleep on the infield of the track. The event will also involve nearly 100 parents. It must run smoothly, and the goal is to get everyone to make it through to the finish. Looking in

from the outside, it is overwhelming to see what has to happen to pull off this challenge. It is one of the reasons why other schools don't do this. It takes a lot of work. Organization, volunteers, the ability to process the big picture and what needs to be done, are key elements to success. If organizers can take on the challenge of the impossible and make it possible, it will be a life changing experience!

As a school, the goal is to get as many students as possible to complete the challenge of the 24 Hour Run. Preparation is in the training and meetings. Once the starting gun goes off, it's up to the students. During the time they are on the track, they will run in coed teams of 12 to 13, much like a relay, with mixed 6th, 7th, and 8th graders. One person will always be on the track running their mile with the team baton, while the next person to run is stationed on the inside edge of the track, timing the current runner. The two people who are next in line are on deck, stationed right behind the timers. When the runners finish, they are told their time, and the timers take the batons and start running. Meanwhile, the first person on deck takes the timer's spot, moving everyone up one position. One

of the most important jobs now is to have the runners that just finished get the next person due to be on their deck. Then the runners log their times. It is the finished runner's responsibility to make sure the next runner is ready to go or their team starts to break down. After their run, they should have just under two hours before they run again. This continues for the entire 24 hours. It's designed so each person should get twelve miles in by the time the event is done. This is all completed on the infield of the track. That's the boundary line, and participants are not allowed to leave except for bathroom breaks in the building.

The sleeping arrangements are simple. However, it's also the biggest concern of the parents. Tents are set up on the infield, which is clearly divided into a boys' side and a girls' side. In the middle of the field, we have a twenty-yard-wide common area where participants can socialize. At no time can the boys cross the line into the girls' tent area, and vice versa, or they go home. If they need to get someone on their team from a restricted area, one of the team captains is used. In theory this should be sufficient, but with hundreds of kids and distractions, hiccups will occur. That is why parents and team leaders are necessary. The team leaders are the first line of defense in solving problems. If they can't solve the problem, then the parent coaches assigned to the team can guide them, but parents are not supposed to do tasks for them. The most common problem is not being able to find the next person in their line. If all else fails, Susie or I will step in. Over the years, our job has gotten more efficient. The students are great, and the parents are awesome at quick fixes, then stepping back. The runners

know their responsibilities and that they are expected to perform. No matter how tired or cold they are, they must get up and do their part without complaints. They know their team is counting on them, and they have a responsibility.

Where do I even start? How do we plan for everything that has to be done? These are the top two questions people ask. For me, it wasn't writing everything down on paper in complete thoughts or in order. I thought about the event for months before I had anything written that was remotely understandable. It was the vision, or the **why** that I worked out first and had to feel good about. It had to be something that would get other people excited. This goes back to the Golden Circle (page 8), but I was doing this before I understood the process. It just worked for me. It was a natural flow. When it came to **how**, it was the process of how everything is going to work. How do we make sure runners can do this for the entire 24 hours? It's the **what** that can drive organizers crazy. This keeps me up at night. I become hyper-focused on the topic and become self-absorbed in the project. If the first two areas are worked out, the **what** falls into place but takes most of the time. The problem is the thoughts and ideas are happening so fast. Organization is the key. To help combat this I start small, like sticky-notes small. Why sticky notes? Because they're quick and easy to move. I'm not worried about organizing yet, I just want to get my ideas down. After a while a pattern or key topics emerge. At that point, making an outline of the key topics will make it easier to fill the gaps and guide organizers through the rest of the details. The other key to

organization is to make sure a timeline of what and when exists. This may start very open and loose but, as the event date draws closer, it becomes very specific and is broken down to the hour or minutes. Everyone prepares themselves differently when it comes to ideas and problem-solving. However, one thing is consistent: Our brains have a tendency to want to solve problems when we're relaxed. The brain sorts through all the information during the day but, when we relax, we are clear headed, uncluttered, and open. Many times, this is when the solution presents itself. This is when leaders need to be ready to save thoughts. Whether it's with old-school pen and paper or the use of technology, get it off your brain so moving on can occur. Statistically this happens most often while driving or trying to sleep. Having a way to record ideas will not only help the organization but it will reduce stress, especially at night when sleep is vital.

Timeline

NUMBER OF STUDENTS (Average)
First meeting – 500+
Permission slip returned – 325-450
Day of the run – 270-450

SCHEDULE

Beginning of year – Get small photos of students (2 sets) from yearbook person or office.

Two weeks before spring break – Print 600 copies, 25 additional log sheets

Week before spring break – Talk about project in class.

Wednesday before spring break – 1st meeting in upper gym, mandatory meeting, to go through packet (just before spring break).

6 weeks of training, check off log sheets every Monday, and talk to the kids before they run.

Week 1 (1/2 mile) – Setting goals, no walking.
Order necessary materials (colored paper, stopwatches, etc.)

Week 2 (3/4 mile) – Physicals, shoes, and goals

Week 3 (1 mile) – Parents' help needed for the event, better mile time?
Do at the same time as the timed mile
Submit open PO for the T-shirts

Week 4 (1 ½ miles) – Pacing, working toward goals, don't wait for Tuesday turn-ins!
Contact media!
Start collecting "entry fee" for shirts, equipment, and supplies.

Week 5 (2 miles) – Getting tougher, integrity, hand in physicals
Prepare bench labels

Week 6 (2 ½ miles) (1 week before event) – Hardest part, pacing, goals, shoes or inserts, mandatory meeting on ***
Tuesday parent meeting, last call for $ and physicals
Reserve tower lights
Order shirts
Fire permit
Cut batons
Purchase last minute equipment
Meet with department
Re-contact media
Friday – split teams
Start labeling teams with photos

Week 7 (1 mile 2x) (week of event)– 1 lap relays in class, explain last training, combine tents, individual questions
Explain the team leaders' role and the meeting at 6 pm the next day
Monday – Post teams in both locker rooms and gym
Finish labeling teams with photos
Review delegated jobs
Prepare for meeting
Organize supplies
Type out team sheets
Send list of participants to teachers & lunch room
Label batons with team color names
Re-label stopwatches
Tent card numbers that need replacing

Tuesday Meeting
Participants (after school until 3:00)
Parents & Volunteers (6:00 – 6:45)
Organize student photos (laminated copy for time log sheets & set for parents)

Day Before Event –To Do
Print shirts
Print team logs (2 copies)
Print team coach sheets (2 copies – one goes in binder for parent volunteer tent)
Line field
Get all equipment down and ready to go
Assemble parent coaching clipboards (two team with photos and shirt color)

Day of Event –To Do
Big top tent 20 x 30 - 8:00
Bleachers - 8:30
Chairs - 8:30
Snow fence - 9:00
Tables
Misc. supply bin
Fire pits & wood
Generators – Noon
Set up lower gym: cones, shirts, batons, attendance, team leader instructions, pencil, marker. – 1:00

Meeting after school on day of event – ½ hour (2:20 – 2:50 in bleachers by teams)

After event
Send out thank you notes to parents
Set up dates for next year's 24 Hour Run

One of the tricks to having a successful program is to think about every scenario and solve problems before they happen. In many cases, this may require having a plan "B." In general, through the years, we have prepared for it all, but the one factor we can't control is the weather. We do what we can and keep the event outside if at all possible. Running inside is the last resort, which we have done. Teenagers rarely wear jackets, but this will be a wake up call for those who think they can just tough it out. It's not so much about bad weather, just poor preparation. That same preparation is needed for running the event. Plan on items breaking, parents and runners not knowing what to do, unwanted visitors, injuries, emotional breakdowns, and a catalogue of scenarios that are not part of a smooth-running event.

"What color is pistachio?" "Is azalea a good color?" "I just don't want to be the same color as last year." These are some of the comments and questions I get when it comes to T-shirt colors. It is the last bit of excitement and mystery before the start. What color are we and what does the design look like? With so many runners on the track and infield, one way to help find your team is by shirt color. These shirts serve several purposes during the 24 Hour Run. The shirts help in finding your team, but more importantly, they help us identify who belongs. If anyone on the track or infield is not wearing the event shirt, they must stay on the outside border of the track. The exception to this is when parents visit or drop off supplies. We always have high school alumni come to visit. With so many participants involved, this is a form of crowd control, and it works pretty well. The shirts are also a way to keep track of the runners' times. They use Sharpies to write their mile times on their shirts, and this is usually a topic of many discussions. They are proud to show off their times and how many miles they have run. The students love to sign each other's shirts. It's kind of like a 24-hour yearbook signing.

1999   2000   2001

2002   2003   2004

2005   2006   2007

2008   2009   2010

2011   2012   2013

2014   2015   2016

Two days before the event I post the teams. Students check the lists to find their team assignments. As much as the participants think they want to be on the same team as their friends, it works out better if they are not. I randomly draw teams that are equal coed with 6th, 7th, and 8th graders. Friends on the same team will have very little chance to talk and hang out because three to four team members will always be at their designated position at the track. Once we get started, they quickly realize this is a non-issue. The only team students are allowed to pick is the elite team. This is a team of 10 instead of the 12 or 13. This elite team is made up of the top runners and most highly motivated kids in the school. This is the team that runs faster and more than any other team. Most, if not all ten, will run 26.2 miles, a marathon, by the finish. They are the "Energizer Bunnies" that just keep on going.

Even after all the planning was done the first year, two problems remained: no budget and questionable school support. The first problem was how to pay for the supplies needed for the event. The school was not about to pitch in, their budget was already tapped out. I literally had to hit the road and raise the funds needed to get the event off the ground. We squeaked by our first year, lighting the track with candles and luminary bags, tiki torches, and glow sticks. It looked awesome, but it took a lot of work to keep them lit, and it really wasn't enough light. Over the years, we've gotten smarter and the parents and community have been awesome. One of the benefits of being in the community for so many years is that we really get to know a lot of families. These connections pay off, especially if the kids learned something and enjoyed class. Even better are the student alumni who manage facilities that have products and/or equipment that are needed. The "Parent Group" now helps fund the event. Local businesses support the program, and parents are more than willing to help with supplies any way they can. There's something to be said about parents whose children have been out of the program for 8 years still coming back to support us with donations and supplies. People want to get involved and help, just ask.

School Equipment Supplied

- Stopwatches (a lot)
- Orange backer-boards for stopwatches
- Log sheets for mile time (1 for each team)
- Batons (1 for each team)
- Big top tent (20 x 30)
- Parent volunteer popup
- Quadrant number
- Fire pits (2)
- Wood & kindling (pickup truck load or full cord)
- Fire permit
- Fire extinguishers (2)
- Lighters (4)
- Generators (2 large tow behind diesel, 1 small)
- Gasoline (1 gallon for small generator)
- Lights (for small generator)
- Folding tables (4)
- Bleachers
- Orange snow fencing (50 yards)
- Garbage cans (4 – 55 gallon drums)
- Garbage bags (20)
- Bull horn
- Black permanent markers (2)
- Box of sharp pencils
- Swiss army knife (you never know)
- Student emergency cards
- First aid kit (1)
- Pre-wrap (3 rolls)
- Athletic tape (10 rolls)
- Ice packs
- Band-Aids
- Antiseptic ointment
- Derma-clear (2 rolls)
- Scissors
- Gauze pads
- Lip balm
- Vaseline
- Shaving razors
- Sunscreen
- Hydrogen peroxide
- Cotton
- Glide anti-friction stick

When the school staff was informed about the program that first year, there was an interesting mix of reactions. Not everyone was on board. Why not? This was going to be one of the coolest events ever, at least from my perspective. Not everyone shared the same vision. The many positive comments and much needed support were helpful, but I was not prepared for the negative comments or the lack of interest by some even in the physical education department. We presented this idea to the staff and told them the event would run from 3:00 PM on Thursday to 3:00 PM on Friday and that some of their students would not be in class Friday because they would be running on the track. The comment that stung the most was, "That will interrupt my class, now I have to deal with those (3 or 4) kids when they get back." I was shocked, hurt, and frustrated by this. These were teachers, why couldn't they see the value of the experience the participants were about to receive. I was disappointed to find that some of them had a problem being flexible for one day. As a physical education teacher, working in spaces that the entire school utilizes, kids are taken out of our classes regularly. My daily teaching has to be flexible. I was frustrated that not everyone saw the value of the event. Instead of defending what we were doing, I had to let it go and just hope the whole event would be worth it and be successful.

How was I going to pull this off if I didn't have support from my department? I would have to work harder! Between negative comments from some of the teachers and the lack of interest from my own department, that little word "no" kept creeping in and fueling a fire in me. I'll show them! Susie Johannesen, one of the other physical

education teachers, was on board; however, there were some in the department who felt it was going to be too much work or that it would not work at all. At one point, I remember telling one of them, "I am prepared to do this without anyone's help or involvement, that's how strongly I feel about the program." That was my determination to stand! Funny what happened—as we got closer to the date, the energy level of the school began changing. A buzz was in the air about what our school was going to do in a few weeks. Two weeks before the event everyone was getting on board. The rest of my department stepped up, and I actually needed the help. We came together as a department and pulled off one of the most amazing experiences our school ever had.

KELLY

I want to prove to my mom that I'm not too small or skinny to do this. I can do this!

Parent & Alumni Teams

Your children will become who you are, so be who you want them to be. —**Unknown**

Parents love this event as much as the students. After the first year or two, parents started asking if they could actually participate. "That would be cool," I thought. This could be a family experience involving the whole community. The trick was how to do this without disrupting the program or taking anything away from the young runners. How could the parents get a similar experience? We decided to have them sign up, train, and make a team, just like the students. We stationed adults and alumni at one corner of the track just on the outside perimeter. This allowed those participants to have some space from the kids and vice versa. Adults set up their area as they saw fit, with chairs, fire pits, tables, etc. We put them on a corner of the track near the road so they could also act as a buffer for security. For the parents, it's like a 24 hour tailgate (without alcohol). Some may be experiencing their first running event while others are seasoned marathon runners. Now that the adult team has been established, we have parents, just like the students, who can't wait for the 24 Hour Run each year. My wife, Trish, is one of them. She has participated in more 24 Hour Runs than anyone else, (which I think is awesome!). Sometimes it's not the parents idea to be part of the event; their children encourage the sign up. One of the best rewards is to hear that parents are motivated. It's great to know a runner has asked a parent to be involved or to run and

help them train. It is not uncommon to hear, "My kid is making me run!" They sense the excitement in their children and they want it too! It's great to hear about families running together, it's important for both sides to support each other. It may seem small, but it's something both parties will remember for years—not only what they did, but how they felt during that time. We hear great stories from parents about how this changed their relationship with their children. It's also fulfilling to hear about couch-potato parents who become inspired and now run marathons because of this community event. Some marathoners feel this event is harder than a marathon because of the start/stop aspect. When parents are this involved in the program, it solidifies the importance of what the event means. The lasting impact it can have on all ages becomes a key component.

The biggest complaints we receive from students who have moved on to high school are about how they don't get to do this event anymore and how much they miss this. So we started thinking: What if they could come back? We couldn't do this while they were in high school because the school administration would question why their kids were missing school to participate in our program. We could, however, allow any former 24 Hour Run participant who was at least eighteen years of age and out of high school (freshman in college) to come back. They would run it just as they did as students and be set up just outside the track the same as parents. Would anyone actually return? If they did, could they still finish? Two months before the event and before we gave out any information to the middle-school students, we had alumni contacting us to get on the alumni team. Every year since, we've had a team return. How cool is it to have former students come back and repeat the event again because they enjoyed it so much the first time! Now whole families can do this event in the same year. It's redeeming to see them return and touch base again on a personal level. We've even had some college students choose to become physical education teachers because of their experience.

As the time draws near for the event, the returnees are just as excited and nervous as the middle-schoolers. Excitement abounds, and they've not even done one mile. At 3:00 PM, with great enthusiasm, the appointed team members start their first lap. Around the halfway point of the event, most returnees remember how tough it was and realize how tough it still is. The test is to see if they remember what it takes to finish. Every year they excel; while some struggle, others fly around the track. The middle-school runners think it's neat that someday they will be able to come back and do this too. One of the special moments the alumni team repeats each year happens during the final lap. They all run together as a group—**only** after being sure all the other runners have finished before them. They are the last to finish the final lap.

ANITA

I've never been so cold, tired, and sore, and had such a great time!

The Day Of ...

Challenges are what make life interesting and overcoming them is what makes life meaningful. —**Joshua Marine**

I cannot sleep; I have been awake for several hours. Now it's time to go to school, my favorite day of the school year is about to begin! My pickup truck is packed for every conceivable weather condition or minor emergency. I'm ready, but are the kids? Arriving at school early, I open the gym doors and prepare for the train of cars and passengers, along with the gear they will be piling along the walls in the gym. Cars are backed up for a quarter-mile with parents ready to drop off their children and enough gear to camp for a week. We try to move everyone along as quickly as possible; I love to see the interaction of the parents and their children as they unpack vehicles. Everyone is excited and nervous at the same time. They can't wait until the end of the day for the 3:00 PM start. Some students bring loaded wagons, while others bring backpacks. Tents, coolers, sleeping bags, pillows, blankets, and stuffed animals are just some of the items they gather up and drag into the school. All belongings are labeled and packed into the gym. Parents say their good-byes in hugs and kisses. Words of encouragement abound, as if they are sending them off to camp.

For the next five hours I will be setting up and delegating what needs to be done on the field. Much organization goes on behind the scenes before and during the special day, and now it all has to come together before we meet with the runners. Unfortunately, this event is not one that can be set up ahead of time. A big top tent is raised, and generator tower lights are erected for the evening. Bleachers are moved, and team log sheets are secured to tables. The field is marked for tents, and the starting line/exchange zone is completed. We move at a fast and furious pace and somehow it always seems to get done in the nick of time before the participants assemble in the gym at the end of the school day.

Everyone is excited. The energy fills the school! Even though students go through the traditional day as usual, their minds are on what will happen after school. They have trained for six weeks and it's finally here. The big question on everyone's mind is, "What do the shirts look like this year?" I keep this information under wraps until the last

minute just to help maintain the suspense. Right after the final school bell, everyone piles into the gym for their final briefing and for the distribution of team shirts. For the first time they get to see what the design looks like and their team's color.

For the next half hour we have to manage the excitement and pump them up at the same time. They are like popcorn popping as they enter the gym, jumping up and down like sprinters do at the starting line to warm up. But they are not warming up, the energy is oozing out of them, and they need a release. Last minute details are given about the weather, their responsibilities, and attendance. We challenge them to focus on their goals, think about the stories we told of others overcoming obstacles, and keep in mind the characteristics of success. We remind them that they are one of the few who have worked hard enough to get to this point. Now is the time to see what they can accomplish. One of my favorite scenes that always gives me a rush is that sea of bodies, all sitting quietly, listening for the last bit of information. After a pause, I yell out, "Let's go!" It hits like a shock wave of energy. In that moment, every year, everyone stands at the same time and cheers before making their way to the track. The energy from the students is about ready to explode, and we just got a small taste. With about ten minutes to spare, they grab all their gear and scramble to their spots anxiously waiting. Then it happens.

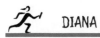 DIANA

I became more ambitious about the things I do. Ever since the 24 Hour Run training started, I've begun to enjoy running even if it's a hard sport, I never want to give up.

I'm not telling you it's going to be easy, I'm telling you it'll be worth it.
—**Art Williams**

The Starting Gun

The starting gun goes off loudly, and the first steps of the journey are taken. We remind the runners to pace themselves; they have a long way to go. They can't seem to help themselves. One would think we were at the horse races the way they explode from the starting line. Like thoroughbreds, they want to run. The adrenaline has kicked in, and can't be contained. The timers and teammates on deck are shaking in anticipation of their turn at the mile. For many, this first mile is a personal record. The excitement and training has paid off, but we are only 1 hour into the event, we have 23 more to go. We have let them know this may be the hardest activity they have ever attempted so they can be as prepared as possible. If they make it through, it will be worth every effort they've gone through to arrive here—and finish.

It is controlled chaos! Hundreds of people all over the field, hauling gear to their spots, setting up tents, and running on the track. For the untrained eye, it seems overwhelming, but this is what we have trained to do. Everyone has a job; they know what to do and when to do it. Our job now is to facilitate, encourage, and handle any small emergencies.

Peace Fire

In the very center of the field, ten people work frantically to start a fire. It is not just any fire, and it's not started by traditional means. A mix of age groups, including alumni and parents, work as a unit to build momentum. If the group cannot work as a team, the fire will never start. They are using a bow drill to ignite the fire. A bow drill uses a small bow and spindle to create friction on the fireboard, creating an ember that will be used to start a fire. This particular one, however, requires ten people to operate.

Dan Creely, a professor at Northeastern Illinois University, has been a friend and mentor for many years. He is unique in his ability to get others to believe in themselves when they would normally have doubts. He is also very spiritual in finding a balance in his own life. Dan came to me with an idea he thought our students would embrace, creating another meaningful connection with the 24 Hour Run. Mr. Creely called it a "Peace Fire," as it was connected to an ancient Peace Fire. I thought it would be a great idea.

However, before we could start our fire, we sought and were granted permission by Nowaten Dale Thomas, a Katchita (spiritual leader) with the Kansas Band Potawatomi Native Americans. This was out of the ordinary, as this eternal sacred fire is steeped in tradition.

In 1996, Nowaten Dale Thomas gave permission for their Misho Skodance (Sacred Fire) to be carried by Muk-ta The Bruce Hardwick and Mukwa-o Day Duane Kinnart to a gathering in Lake Geneva, Wisconsin. These Fires have burned for thousands of years and were only used by his people. What makes the Fire special is not only how it's started and tended, but that coals from the previous Peace Fires are introduced to each new Fire. These coal bundles, wrapped in a small red cloth and tied with white string, represent the collective consciousness of all the participants who have ever gathered. Nowaten knew it was time this Fire should be shared with all humanity. Dan spoke to Nowaten about bringing the Fire to our 24 Hour Run. He described the challenge our students would be facing and why they were accepting this challenge. Nowaten was a paratrooper in the 82nd Airborne, and he served in the Korean War. He understood the principles of dedication, commitment, and sacrifice. Nowaten liked the idea and was honored that the students would share in his tradition with their Fire.

The 10-person bow drill was made and sized for adults so the students were challenged from the very beginning. They had to make adjustments, but they were determined. Under Dan's directions, all ten people had to work together as if they were one. They needed to create a single spark from the friction of the twisting five-foot spindle to ignite the cedar dust. The first attempt was unsuccessful, we weren't even close. The crowd wondered, "Will this really work?" Tired and breathing hard the group refocused for a second try. It is a unique feeling to realize the power of the group, creating an intense rhythm, working harder as a group than one can as an individual. They found a rhythm, focused their efforts, and smoke began to billow from the fireboard again. Mr. Creely said, "Pretend you are driving a car and you just pulled out of a parking space onto the street. Keep your rhythm the same, as you pull onto the expressway. Pick up your speed and keep going for 50 more strokes." Everyone was straining, but no one wanted to quit. Students stepped in to relieve exhausted friends without missing a beat. The base of the bow drill billowed clouds of smoke. It had to be working! Quickly and carefully we dismantled the bow drill and watched Mr. Creely gently collect the ember on a piece of Birch bark. He delicately placed the ember on a nest of jute. (Three-inch pieces of jute twine were pulled apart and shredded by the participants before they left the gym to come outside. This contribution made everyone a part of the experience of starting the fire.) With a few gentle, long, slow breaths the jute erupted into flame. There was a gasp and cheers from the students. The small nest was added to the big jute nest from all the students. We had our Fire for the 24 Hour Run, a Peace Fire. The students realized they were part of something bigger than themselves—something they could not have done on their own. This powerful experience defined the beginning of our 24 Hour Run. The ripple effect from our run and what Nowaten shared about the Fire was realized. Dan Creely Jr. sent Nowaten Dale Thomas the story and photos of our 24 Hour Run and the success of the Peace Fire. He had been battling for his health for some time and was reaching the end of his life. Upon hearing of the letter, Nowaten smiled and said, "This is a good thing" to his wife. Two weeks after our event, Nowaten passed into his own Spirit World.

Once the fire is lit, it is up to the runners to tend the fire throughout the event. Something about this fire is different than those in the other fire pits. The students do a great job, a sense of respect and care for this fire is evident. A few days after the event, we make hundreds of our own coal bundles from the coals of the sacred Peace Fire. These bundles have been taken to locations throughout the world to be left in a special place where "you know" it belongs, given to someone else, added to a ceremony, or placed in another Peace Fire. Many runners hold onto their coal as a token of their experience.

Bringing spirituality into the picture can be problematic, and I wasn't sure how this next idea was going to be received. For the Native Americans, the Peace Fire is a connection to the Spirit World. This connection is made by the offering of tobacco to give thanks and carry intentions to the Spirit World. When tobacco is placed in the fire, the smoke connects to the world of the Spirit. Students are given the option of taking a pinch of tobacco from a wooden bowl to the Peace Fire and, after a moment of silence, tossing it into the fire. We do not make a big deal out of this and try not to make anyone uncomfortable. Honestly, at first I thought we might get some negative feedback from parents or administration. But it was just the opposite. People embrace the process and want to be a part of the Peace Fire in their own way. Parents and even our principal share in the experience. People respect the space, take a moment to themselves, and feel good about the Peace Fire being part of their event.

Months after incorporating the Peace Fire into the 24 Hour Run, I was looking on the internet for a topographical view of our school, Lundahl's property. I couldn't believe what I found! On Google Earth, from over 200 miles up, there was a satellite photo taken during our 24 Hour Run. It was a perfect shot of the grounds. You could see runners on the track, the grid on the field with all the tents, and in the very center, our Peace Fire. It gave me goose bumps knowing that Nawaten once shared how this Peace Fire would touch the world!

A PROUD MOM

My son watched Lundahl do the 24 Hour Run for years. On his last day of 5th grade, I got him a tent to use the next year in his first 24 hour run. He was born with a heart condition he eventually outgrew. However a year later he was needing breathing treatments multiple times everyday. He never allowed this to slow him down. And today I proudly watched the most courageous, determined boy successfully achieve his goal of 26.2 miles.

41

Challenges are really just a test to see how much you deserve success. —**Joel Brown**

Tent City

The infield of the track is littered with runners, gear, and tents as students stake their claims. The boys' and girls' sides are spray painted in grids and numbered so we can later find runners who are crashed in their tents. As the first-milers are on the track, just about everyone else is trying to find the best spot for the next 24 hours. For many, setting up their tent is a learning experience, and it's meant to be. Parents are not allowed to set up beforehand. We want the students to do the work. Some struggle for hours and find they have missing parts, while others set up in minutes. Either way, everyone is having a good time, and they are all in it together. We generally end up with 60 to 75 tents on the infield. It's surprising to see what shows up every year—such a variety of brands, styles, and sizes. We have seen everything from Scout tents from the 70s, one-person tents, and multi-room tents with wings one could almost live in. The trick is to convince students to

get as many people as possible in each tent. This reduces the number of tents we have to search, looking for individuals. Teams also have a better chance of knowing where their teammates are. If they have a six-person tent, we want them to shoot for eight people. Most everyone does a great job of packing everyone in but, once in a while, we find

a person who doesn't have a place to sleep. This is usually one of the quietest people in the group and/or one that may not have any friends participating in the run. They try to keep calm, but we can see they are worried, in a bit of a panic, about not having a place to sleep. One of the interesting side effects of this event is that many of the barriers between students are torn down. They meet new people, they socialize with other grade levels, everyone is helping and sharing and working for a common goal. When we look for a tent with some spare room and ask if they can take in one more person, there has never been any hesitation. It is awesome to see the students step up and do what is right.

Cell Phones

Technology has changed the students and this event more than anything else. The first year of the 24 Hour Run, myself and two other parents were the only people with cell phones. Now everyone has one.

They've been great for timing and listening to music to help keep the students motivated, but they also come at a cost. One of the best learning experiences infused in the program those first few years was to plan and be prepared. When we started the event, we made sure we had everything needed to last the entire time. This planning included

food, warmer clothes, extra shoelaces, etcetera. This was suppose to be one of those learning experiences that students didn't realize they were going through. Now, if students forget something, they call home and have their parents drop it off. That learning experience, about how to be prepared, is vanishing to some degree. We could never ask the kids not to bring their phone, that would be a liability. Leaving their phones at home is like going through drug withdrawals—it can take up to two days before people can function effectively without them. We only have 24 hours. So we came up with a challenge. During this first hour we come around with paper lunch bags. Anyone interested in seeing if they can make it through the event without their phone, can put their phone in the bag and staple it shut. Giving it back to them is the key. It is now up to them to see if they have the strength to leave their phone alone—if they can make it through without tearing into the bag. Most don't even want to try, but there are a couple dozen who will. This is torture for some, but we do get a handful that succeed. The ones who make it feel great about doing so, because they know they truly did it on their own and were prepared for the event.

BRIAN

This is a grandparent moment! When asked what that meant he explained: This is one of those times when I'm a grandparent I'll be able to tell my grandkids, this is what I did when I was your age in middle school!

If no one thinks you can, then you have to. —**Marlen Esparza**

You're on Your Own

It is impressive to see all the tents, the students running, and the fleet of cars pulled up close to the track and filling the outfield and parking lot. This is the busiest time of the event, and everyone wants to stop by. Parents are getting off work and dropping off last minute supplies, siblings are envious, and high school kids are trying to pay a visit and reminisce about the time they were here. As much as we love to have everyone come by, we still have to manage the event, and the event is for our students. It is time to cut off visitors and close the infield. If someone is not wearing a 24 Hour Run shirt, they are not allowed on the infield. We have a small section of bleachers on the outside of the track where people can watch and cheer. It is not easy to ask friends and siblings to move to the outer edge, but we ask them to respect the event and to understand this is the participant's time. We encourage parents to keep their visits short. Many make a quick check and leave it at that; they get it. Let the kids do their time without the parents hovering over them, and let them grow. However, occasionally we have some that hang out with the students, set up camp with them, then settle in as if they are part of the event. It is never fun to ask parents to give their kids some space in this situation. We love the support and

the fact that the parents are taking an interest in what their children are doing. If they want to spend more time at the event, we encourage them to help by volunteering or joining the adult running team. This is for the students, we need to let them be kids, make mistakes, learn on their

own, and have success knowing they did it themselves. Soon families thin out and head home, now the students are on their own to achieve their goals.

🏃 ARIANNA

My favorite memory was probably when I had to run at 2:30 in the morning in 43 degree weather! That was fun. But I really liked watching my friends accomplish amazing things and becoming better people right there.

A goal is a dream with a deadline. —**Napoleon Hill**

Goals

Through the years, we notice that students are not only doing awesome in the event, but they are achieving more than expected. Somehow this is challenging them in ways I never thought about, it becomes personal. They are not just doing this to see if they can finish, they are doing this because they have something to prove. It's great when teachers can get someone to do this, but it is even better when students have a hidden agenda that motivates them personally. We want to help the students reach their goals and maybe focus a little more on why they are out here.

The addition of "My goal is. . ." on their log sheet shifted the intensity of the event. As mentioned before, by writing their goal down then looking at it everyday, they have an 86% chance of achieving it. So what better place to put it than on their log sheet that they look at several times every week? At first, we just hoped for goals such as running "x" amount of miles or under a certain time, or goals that added focus or cause. As I check their progress each week, I read their goals. Many are the standard goals we anticipate, like more miles than last year or better times. But some are very personal, touching, insightful, and/or emotional. I want everyone to reach their goal, but the odds are against me, so how many students can I help? It turns out most of the students are well on their way without any additional help. They are learning what it takes to

set a goal, how to take steps toward it, and how to follow through. We just have to give them a gentle nudge. For many their dream, or goal, has a deadline at 3:00 PM on Friday.

Samplings of students' goals follow:

- To show I'm something other than a couch potato! — Emma
- To get good exercise and start running with my dad. —Dylan
- To run a marathon (26.2 miles) during the 24 Hour Run. —Corryn
- To prove running is a great sport and that I'm capable of anything. Also learn not to stress or freak in hard situations but enjoy them. —Chelsea
- To never doubt myself and to run for 24 hours. —Natalie
- Stay motivated; believe in myself. —McKenna
- To beat my brothers mile time of 5:58. —Savannah
- To run at least 5 separate miles under the time of 6:30. —Connor
- To succeed in spite of my diabetes. —Matthew
- To be a successful team leader. —Mariano
- Get good sleep in and eat good food and no phone use. —Hailey
- To get more exercise and get in shape. —Amanda
- To get better physically and mentally. —Grace
- Not to let asthma get in my way to do this. —Amy
- To make it through the run without passing out. —Becca
- To be more responsible and live a healthier life. —Samantha
- To become the "Elite Team" leader. —Cameron
- To prove to my parents that I can get in shape enough to join high school football. —Mark
- To prove my heart is strong enough after having open heart surgery when I was younger. —Jen

ANONYMOUS

My goal is to prove my physical therapist wrong and run even though I will probably need surgery on my feet, knees, and lower back in my early 20s.

7:00 PM

Campfires with friends: The best therapy ever! —**Fred Kaiser**

Fire Pits

Something about a campfire brings people together. Bundling up in cool weather and relaxing with friends feels great. Students can talk and "hang out" without worrying about it getting late and having to go home. The campfire is one of those experiences students look forward to each year. The question is always, "When can you light the fire pits?" Some years we have to ration the firewood because we can easily go through a full pickup truck load. Depending on conditions, we could go through even more. We look to the parents for help with the firewood supply. Every year, they come through. Some donate their stockpile, others work for a business that can donate wood. Some years, one family will buy a cord of wood for the event. Once the fire pits are lit, everyone settles in for the long night ahead. They gather up chairs and blankets and pick a spot with their friends. The "8th grade fire" is always furthest away from the start/finish line, they seem to want their space and claim their territory. The 6th and 7th graders don't care, they are just glad to have a fire to sit around. There is lots of laughing, singing, and people trading stories as they await their turn to be on deck.

There are two rules we have to enforce that parents appreciate and students hate. There is no snuggling or sleeping at the fire pits. Parents get nervous when they see the young ones all bundled up and getting comfortable together. Rightfully so. As much as they may want to spend this once-in-a-lifetime event together, we can't endorse any "public display of affection." They don't like it when we ask them to find their own seats, but they respect the request. What is more difficult and dangerous is when someone falls asleep at the fire pit. This is a safety concern!

Nice and warm, exhausted, and all comfy, your body and eyes get very, very heavy. As much as students may want to stay awake, when they lay down, it is almost impossible. The accident we never want is for hot coals to spark and start a sleeping student's blanket on fire. The other drawback is we cannot find sleeping students buried under blankets at the fire pit, instead of in their tents. The rule is if one is laying down or asleep, one is sent back to one's tent. When runners are that tired, they need some sleep time in their tent. We can find them there. This is tough for some of participants—as soon as they are awakened, they say, "I'm up, I'm up!" The last thing they want is to leave the comfort of the fire. But it's too late. It is time for them to hunker down in their own tent. In the end, this keeps the snuggling under control, gets them the sleep they need, and keeps everyone safe.

Fundraiser

Around this time I get a popular question from some of the new parents to the program. "Why isn't this a fundraiser, you could raise a lot of money." I am not against raising money for a great cause, but sometimes the cause can become intrinsic motivation. This is important, because **there will come a time in their life when they just need to do something without any reward other than the satisfaction of overcoming adversity**. It is important to learn how to do this because it is easy to give up when the going gets tough. Students need to understand that it is easier to keep going than it is to start over. Runners learn that during this event. Schools and the community have other great fundraisers. I feel that the students, and myself, have so much to do to prepare for the run that adding something else would distract from the lessons and goals of the 24 Hour Run. By the time we finish our conversation, folks understand why it's organized in this way. In fact, we have more support because the students are doing this event purely to see if they can—**intrinsic motivation**.

 TAYLOR

My favorite things are talking by the fire all night until the sun comes up and laughing even with people I don't know!

*I could conquer the world if only I had
enough ribbon.* —**Napoleon Bonaparte**

Team Leaders

By now the fire pits are lit, everyone has put in a few miles, and campsites are set. Everyone's into a rhythm, and the reality of their challenge sets in. The experience is still new for many and everyone is doing his/her part but, every once in a while, we have a wrinkle. It is the job of the team leaders to step up and help their teams with these minor difficulties. As mentioned earlier, they are the stopgap before the parent coaches or teachers step in and help. As the event has grown, it is easier to get lost in the crowd, literally. So the plan is to enlist a little help from students. At first we selected the leaders for each team based on how well we felt they could take on the responsibility without complaining or shirking the job. We were not sure if middle-school students would want this title—that it might not be "cool." But they do. They feel honored to have the responsibility. Everyone likes to be

recognized for his/her efforts and hold responsibility, a ribbon symbolizes that. The modern military awards their soldiers with military ribbons of distinction just as Napoleon did, so we do the same. We are not treating them like soldiers, but they do get their version of a "ribbon"—a bright green (boys) or yellow (girls) bandana. This is something tangible and they wear it proudly. This distinction is one students ask for and choose as their goal. It is great to see that they want to help and be leaders during a time when they themselves are being tested and pushed to the limit. I find it interesting that those who wish to be leaders are the students we probably would have chosen originally. Maybe it's a position they have a desire to do because they instinctively know they can handle the job. Although the honor is generally reserved for an 8th grade male and female on each team, we occasionally give it to a 7th grader who shows an aptitude as a leader. When that happens, the students are very excited and proud. Sometimes leaders get frustrated when they get called on in the middle of the night to help. They don't quit, however, because they know people are counting on them to keep their team together. It would be interesting to know what these leaders are doing in fifteen years and if they are in a leadership role in their job or life.

 CORRYN

As a team leader, it was frustrating to me how people would not get up out of the tent when I told them it was their turn to run, but when Mr. Kaiser told them, they would just pop up and go.

The darkest nights produce the brightest stars. —**John Green**

I'm Afraid of the Dark

For many, 9:00 PM is their bedtime at home. Not tonight. Too much activity is going on, and too many people want to hang out. It is rare to get any sleep this early in the evening. It will just have to wait. By now everyone has moved into tents and some are proud to show them off. They like to give tours as if it were their first home. It's like the ultimate fort, and some are trying to outdo others. The activity level in the common area has leveled off, and the running around is down to a slumbering walk. Many realize they need to conserve energy. When students are not at their posts, they are usually at their tents or the fire pits. This is when the realization sets in that they are on their own, without their parents. Most don't have a problem with this, but for others, fear surfaces.

The first time this situation came up, I was taken aback by the parent's comment: "My daughter is deathly afraid of the dark; she wants to go home." I didn't know what to do at first. In a panic my brain raced to decide if this was a joke or if she was serious. Who signs up for an event, knowing it's going to run all night, when they are afraid of the dark? I had to think about what to say and tread lightly as the daughter's head was buried in her mom's side as she held on in a tight hug.

"Anna, what's going on?" I asked.

"I want to go home," Anna responded. I made two decisions at once: Get her away from her mom and take her someplace well lit. I asked her to come with me for a minute, and I told her mom we would be right back. For a 6th grader and first time runner, this experience

can be overwhelming, but if we just let them go home, they haven't learned anything. My goal was to help her feel safe and keep her in the event somehow. I had to admit, the backside of the track is bordered by a line of trees that is very dark and can be creepy, even for an adult. However, we were taking precautions with tower generator lights and people stationed at key points on the track. We talked about options like coming into the building to take a break, taking a light with her as she ran, or running with a buddy or even myself. After some time sitting on the floor in the school's entry, she decided to go back out and give it a try. When we emerged, her mother thanked me—realizing I had very casually, yet purposely separated the two of them. Anna's mother said she had a tough time when I pulled her daughter aside to talk without her; however, she understood why and gave us the needed space. I didn't talk to Anna again for several hours, and when I caught up with her, she was laughing with friends in a tent and said she was fine. Finding comfort in friends is a powerful source of strength when we need it most—lesson learned.

By stepping back and giving Anna some room to make her own decisions, without the comfort of her parents, we were able to refocus her efforts as to why she was there. A parent's natural instinct is to swoop in and protect, but sometimes we have to help our children learn to fly on their own. This kind of event may be the first test for some parents. Some will hover and not let their child out of their sight. While others will never even stop to check on their child. Somewhere in the middle is a delicate dance we aim for in the relationship. This event may establish new boundaries and encourage branching out into new territories, which is good for both parent and child.

GIANNA

When I start seeing kids running around the neighborhood, I know it's that time of year again. I get this happy feeling inside, knowing how excited they are and how proud they are going to be after they finish. It's the best 24 hours of their life!

*Whether you think you can, or you think you can't,
you're right.* —**Henry Ford**

Confidence

The first mental test of the event is in the training. For most, the two-mile and two-and-a-half mile markers are the furthest students have ever run without walking or stopping. These distances get them mentally prepared for the fatigue and tiredness they will feel, and are designed to replicate what one mile will feel like at 4:00 AM. This is the hump they have to get over. The above quote becomes especially true. The trick is to make sure we encourage runners: "You can do this!" Even in training at school, a few students look to us with anguish etched on their faces. They fight back tears, hoping we will ask them if they are okay or if they would like to rest. They are looking for permission to stop. We must make them believe they can continue. We encourage them: "You are doing great, just keep on going. You are almost done." Nearly every time these runners make it through. They just need someone to show confidence in them when they momentarily lose confidence in themselves.

Eating Right

Food is not a taste test, but a buffet. Nobody is going to starve during the time away from home. Coolers are rolled in, packed with drinks, sandwiches, fruit, GORP, energy bars, and a variety of tasty morsels to hold them over until the next meal. At first, my hope was to feed the participants through donations during the event. That, however, is a monumental task in itself. We try to supply fruit during their time with us, but it is up to them to supply what they need. Although we don't tell them what to eat or put them on a plan, we do suggest they really think about what they are putting into their bodies the days before and during

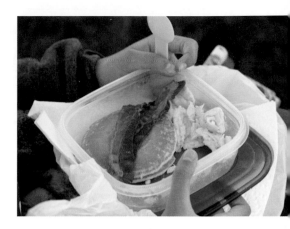

the event. This is something inexperienced runners don't always think about. It can really make a difference in their performance and recovery. They must use some commonsense about when, how much, and what they eat. We find them in their tents with stomach aches if they don't. Occasionally, this still happens but it is quickly remedied with some water and something nutritious to eat. The young runners usually do a great job of packing right. I'm still amazed by how much food is consumed by middle-school students. Many want to show us what they brought. They take pride in knowing they packed well. It's rewarding to see them off the junk food and taking an interest in healthy choices. They learn about what they are putting into their bodies and how it affects them. Parents still drop by to supply them with sub sandwiches, but gone are the days of donuts and coffee drinks. It is not just about the running, but more about what it takes to be healthy during this run and future activities.

 VINCE

It was so funny to me when I would go wake the kids up in their tents and they were so tired and confused they could not remember how to get out of their tent!

Throw me to the wolves, and I'll return leading the pack. —**Unknown**

Blisters

It's amazing to see what some students wear on their feet during physical education classes; it explains why their running gaits are so off. Proper shoes for class are mandatory. The variety and conditions of footwear is mind-boggling. We repeatedly address the importance of appropriate shoes for the 24 Hour Run. They must have shoes that are made for running, are recently broken in before the event, and have good support. The one injury they don't want is a blister, especially early on. "Hot spots" (an area that has friction on the foot before a blister forms) are addressed, taking care of potential problems before they become bigger. One item I carry to use at a moment's notice is Dermiclear anti-friction tape. This material is awesome! I've used it ever since my initial athletic training days in college. It protects feet from blisters. When a blister does erupt, putting a strip of this tape over it can make it feel like it's not even there. No matter how great the precautions, all the running and time on their feet will still produce blisters for some. The trick is to get it before it forms a blister. Middle-schoolers do a good job of this but, once in a while, we get a bloody blister. These take some extra attention, but I have never had anyone drop out because of a blister, no matter how bad it was. Somehow they make it through. It would take more than a blister to take them out of the run.

Determination to Stand

Just when we think everything is on a roll, we find out it's not. A blister could take someone out, but what if their own parents do! A story I am forever proud of includes both the student and parent. Making my rounds, I came across a mother and her daughter, Natalie, having a heated conversation. In my attempt to make sure everything was alright, I discovered Natalie's mom was not there to support her, but to take her home.

When I asked if everything was alright, her mom confronted me saying, "This event is way too stressful on the kids, and this much running is not good for them. I want to take my daughter home, this is too tough for her!" By then the daughter was crying and angry with her mother. Trying to defuse the situation, I asked to speak to the mother away from her daughter. I tried to provide support for the program and the benefits that came from participation, but Mom wanted nothing to do with my reasoning. She again questioned the validity of the event as if she had heard nothing I just said.

I paused, took a deep breath, and said, "Give Natalie a chance; let's see what she can do. If it's not working, then we can visit that problem when it comes. But we are still early in the run, and she's doing great."

Right about that time, Natalie came back into the picture with, "I've trained for this, I can do this, I'm not going home!" Natalie was showing her **Determination to Stand**, one of the characteristics of success that we talk about with the students. However, the temperature of this conversation was a little more heated than I was comfortable

with. Understandably, Natalie's Mom wanted to protect her daughter, but this would have been a better conversation to have weeks ago when she was preparing for the run. I could tell people were watching and listening to how this was unfolding. I had to resolve this soon. Even though I tried to mediate the verbal battle, I was not getting anywhere.

The timing of another mom was perfect. A parent who did not know Natalie's mom put her arm around her. She spoke softly to her as she led her away from the scene. I took Natalie, got her calmed down, and had friends stay with her for support and comfort. After that, I did not speak to the mom again, but she gave Natalie space even though she stayed in her car and watched the rest of the night. Later the next morning I saw Natalie and her mom talking again. This time it was different. Both were smiling and getting along. Natalie was still doing well and showing no signs of fatigue. Mom was now supporting her!

When I checked in with Natalie's mom, she said, "I can't believe what my daughter has been able to do. I get it now, thank you."

I said, "Thanks for giving her a chance, she's doing great! How are you?"

With tears in her eyes, she said, "Good." Now, I don't know what was said to her by one of the other moms, or if it was the chance to step back and watch her daughter from a distance, but this was not the same mom I met six hours earlier. For the rest of the event, Natalie's mom supported her daughter, but at a distance. I am proud of the two of them for what they overcame: Natalie, for her determination to stand for what she believed and for her mom for letting her little girl become a young adult. These conversations were not easy, but it was worth it for both of them in the end.

ANONYMOUS

The best part was having all my friends by my side running with me and supporting me all the way.

Stop watching and start doing. —**Unknown**

Curious Spectators

"Do you know where your kids are? We do, and we would like for you to come pick them up." Every once in a while we have some curious spectators show up that are not involved in the 24 Hour Run. They mean no harm, they're just curious. In the middle of the night, a couple of middle-school students sneak out of the house to check out the event. They lay low on the sidelines of the track, like lions sneaking up to a herd of gazelles. But the attack never happens. They just sit quietly looking for people they know running on the track. The student observers don't try to disturb anything, in fact they do not want to be noticed. They know they are not supposed to be there. With parents patrolling the boundary, and kids ready and willing to sound the alarm if anything out of the ordinary is going on, they are soon spotted. I make my way over to see if I know who they are. I let them know it's great they want to support friends, but they are not allowed to be on school property. They rarely scatter. In fact, they want to have a conversation and just hang out. For them it's "cool" to sneak out and check out the event. They are not expecting me to call their parents to pick them up. They are on school grounds after curfew. I have to make the call. A

little disoriented and confused about why the school is calling them at this hour, I fill their parents in on our uninvited support crew. I sit with them in the parking lot, waiting for the parents to collect their late-night explorers. As a car slowly pulls up, the window rolls down. This is one of those moments when I'm sure parents don't really want to see me. I am sure it could be embarrassing for some parents, but we try not to make a big deal about the visit. We let the parents know that no one is upset and they are not in trouble. We just can't have them here now; they are welcome back in the morning just before school starts. Now, if all our visitors could be like this, it would be an easy night, but in the twilight of the morning, we have had some that were not so accommodating. That's when I needed the help of parents to control the situation.

STEPHANIE

It's great when I'm running and I hear people cheering for me. Also when a lot of people wanted to sign my shirt. It made me feel like I belonged here.

Be the mentor you wish you had. —**Unknown**

Parent Volunteers

I cannot express enough thanks to all the parents over the years that helped this event become so powerful. With 300 to 450 contestants on the infield of the track, we must make sure everyone is where they are supposed to be. It takes more than a couple of people to run this event successfully. Over the duration of the event, we have support from 75 to 100 parents. It's great to see the families support their young ones and the program. Many parents are as enthusiastic as the kids. Vacation days are saved and schedules arranged at work to make sure they are available to help. Some even take the day off, last minute, because they were involved early on in some aspect of the event. They don't want to leave. Either way, it is awesome to have the help. Some sign up for specific hours to assist as a "coach" for a team. Those who need to get home to prepare for work the next morning stay until the last possible moment. They want to be a part of this bonding experience with their own children and other parents, to share in the experience of the 24 Hour Run. We also have the die-hards that commit for the entire 24 hours. These parents hold a special place with me because it's more than a commitment of time—it's the sacrifice of no sleep, being cold, being on the go, and providing help at a moment's notice. Many figure if their children can give something up and struggle for something worth working hard for, then they can do the same. Some need a caffeine buzz to get them through; others feed off the energy from the runners. Every once in a while, we have parents who go above and beyond. They take on responsibilities to do what needs to be done or lead new parent volunteers as they start their rotations. I recall one parent in particular who seemed to push himself each year beyond what I would ever ask for.

When we have our first meeting with students who

want to be part of this event, I share stories of great physical feats. I also talk about some of the tests Native Americans endure to become warriors in their tribe. Tests of honor, integrity, passion, and strength are necessary. I tell them about young Native Americans who have to stand barefoot in the dirt at the highest point in the village, facing West, watching the sunset on the horizon. Once the sun has set, they turn, face East, and wait for the sun to rise. As if that was not hard enough, future warriors would have to do this without disturbing the dirt beneath their feet. The elders of the tribe would check, and if any soil had been moved by their feet, they would not become a warrior of that tribe. Tony Calabrese (who introduced me to the 24 hour run idea) is the only person I know who has done this several times; once, standing in shorts in 40 degree weather just to test himself.

I'm not sure if Mark Adams, the parent I referred to earlier, heard this story I shared with the runners; however, he seemed to test himself each year as he helped with the run. Although he didn't stay in one place without moving, Mr. Adams never sat down or moved from his post (except for bathroom breaks) for the entire 24 hours! Now I stay up for 36 hours straight because I teach the day of the event, set up, and then challenge myself to stay awake to be available for the runners. The trick, for me, is to keep moving. I can't imagine how tough it is to stand in relatively the same spot the entire time. He did this each year he helped. My gratitude goes out to him for being that pillar of strength and commitment. He is a warrior in my mind.

Most of those who work the entire run will tell you it is their favorite day of the year. I think it is amazing that parents support and sacrifice to be a part of this program. It is encouraging and helpful to have these seasoned pros come back over the years. They teach new parents what to expect and how to handle their responsibilities. They also help field a lot of questions and possible doubts about the program. These returning parents are our biggest advocates and supporters. We know we are doing

something right when parents whose children no longer attend Lundahl return to help.

A couple of families stand out in their dedication to the run. The Ventrella and Kirby families are some of our biggest supporters. I first spoke with Mr. Ventrella about physical education class, not about the event. He asked that his daughter be switched from one physical education unit to another because she was better skilled in that sport. We talked about providing variety and experience for his daughter, and that staying in the class would be good for her. He very reluctantly left things as they were, and his daughter enjoyed the class and did well. When the Ventrellas signed up to help the entire 24 hours of the event, I was a little concerned that we might disagree on something else. As most new parents, they were unsure about their assigned jobs; however, as the hours passed, their enthusiasm grew, not just for their own daughters, but for everyone. They had so much energy! They became fully invested in the program and helped with food donations. If I had ask them to take over, I think they would have in a heart beat. Their last year to have a child participating in the event we were sad the Ventrellas would be gone. How could we replace them? As it turned out, we didn't have to just yet. They came back and helped for a couple more years even after their daughters had moved on to high school. They were not just attending for their children, they volunteered for all the participants. After a number of years, we were surprised one night during the event. The entire Ventrella family came back to visit. Their daughters were now in college, but they knew the event was going on, and they had to stop by. We greeted each other with open arms and hugs. We all missed those former times. The family continues to come by, check in, and say "Hi" over the years. That's success!

Donald Kirby is one of those parents who is willing to do anything to help a program or individuals that he believes in. Both his sons

participated in the 24 Hour Run. He was available to help each year. He still contributes—eight years and counting after his youngsters left the program. He believes this experience helped his children succeed in college and as young adults. It is awesome to believe that may be true. From what I know about the family, they were already well on their way to succeed. Mr. Kirby continues to supply the event with food and water contributions from local business. Cases of fruit are made available and the kids inhale the oranges and bananas. It's rare to find someone like Mr. Kirby who helps even when his family is no longer directly involved. Mr. Kirby's business also sponsors my son's passion for ski jumping, as he travels around the country and Europe to pursue his goal of trying out for the Olympic team. I am glad to know him and that we have become friends.

Every contribution counts. It shows that parents want to support such a program. Parents bring pizzas from their restaurants, coffee for all the parents standing in the cold, and other goods. They will gladly bring firewood from their own houses or bring a fire pit to use. Some brought emergency spotlights when ours gave out. They'll contribute just about anything else we could ask for. They want to help. The parents are truly what helps make this event successful!

🏃 **ANONYMOUS**

You hear some random conversations outside your tent when you're trying to fall asleep.

If it's important to you you'll find a way.
If not you'll find an excuse. —**Jim Rohn**

The Night Sky

By now our eyes have adjusted to the darkness that covers the night. The exchange area is well lit, and it is amazing how well we can see with very little light as we walk around the field of tents and fire pits in the common area. We can see runners and team shirt colors. However, we don't always see tent stakes and cords that seem to jump out of nowhere to trip us up.

Over the years, we've had clear night skies exposing stars burning brightly. One can't stop staring at them. Students sit in their chairs looking up, discovering stars and constellations for what seems like the first time. They watch for shooting stars and find satellites orbiting overhead. I am always amazed at the amount of light a full moon reflects. The visibility is surreal, as if a spotlight is on in the distance—no flashlight needed. That night-light in the sky overhead helps guide the participants through their run.

The only time runners are allowed to leave the track to use the bathrooms in the school. It is only about thirty yards from the track area, but when one walks inside after being in the darkness of the night, it's like walking out of a movie theater in the middle of the day. It takes a minute to make the adjustment. Everyone squints as they enter the building, but when leaving, it's back to the reality of the cool, dark night and the challenge ahead.

June Bugs

The lack of light can be stressful or scary. When we hear constant screaming, however, we know something else is going on—June bugs. The 24 Hour Run is always held on the Thursday/Friday of Memorial Day weekend in May. We experienced one of the worst infestations ever in one of our first years. There were so many June bugs the students could not run the track without crushing several. They are harmless beetles that move slowly and are attracted to light. That year, it felt like a plague or swarm had landed at our location. Although most of the runners could handle them on the ground, when they landed in their hair it really freaked them out. Participants, sitting quietly at their timing station, would all of a sudden stand up, screaming and thrashing about as if they were on fire, trying to get the beetle out of their hair. June bugs are not very well balanced creatures, but their legs do

a great job of gripping anything, including clothing and hair. Just when we thought it could not get worse, they started cooking in the lights. The few portable construction lights we had around seemed to be collecting them on the lens of the super hot halogen bulbs. They were frying, smoking, and popping, which was either very "cool" and interesting or completely gross. No one planned for this; it was just one of those times everyone had to roll with and tolerate. We knew nothing else could be done. Thankfully, the torture only lasted a few hours then subsided. They show up every year, but we have never been attacked like that again.

We Can't Find . . .

Now is my turn to go on the attack. I'm looking for participants gone missing! "We cannot find Ben!" one of the parents says to me. Normally when a child goes missing and cannot be found an understandable response is concern. However, the runners know they are required to stay on the infield of the track or be sent home. Unless Ben is in the bathroom, he is within sixty yards of where we are standing in the middle of the football field. He is not missing, we just can't find him. We are running out of time. It is Ben's turn to be on deck, or timing the next runner, and he is not at his post. By this time, the next person in line to find him is the team leader, followed by the parent coach but neither can find Ben. My first question seems obvious, "Did you look in his tent?" The answer is "Yes." This is where the parents must step back and let me do the dirty work.

A funny behavior shows up around this time of night. Everyone is cold and tired. They do anything to find comfort. I locate his tent and call his name. No answer. I shine the light in his tent and peek through the screen door. All I see are piles of blankets, food wrappers, water bottles, and other camp necessities. So I go in to investigate, just to be sure. It looks obvious that he's not here. These youngsters are like small burrowing animals, and this happens every year! Just because we don't see the runner doesn't mean s/he is not there. I pat down the blankets and clothes in the corner, and that's when I find a leg.

"Ben, it's your turn to run, you have to get up!" I say with confidence and urgency. Ben pops up from under the pile of blankets, ready to go.

The parent coach is surprised to see him, "I checked the tent!"

Losing kids in the night is tough, and we have a long way to go. It gets worse before it gets better. Some sleepwalk when awakened. It can get really interesting and funny.

🏃 JENNY

My face is as tired as my legs from laughing and smiling with my friends all night.

*No matter how slow you go, you are still lapping
everybody on the couch.* —**Unknown**

Halfway Done

The 24 hour clock sits across the track facing the timers counting down the seconds until it reaches zero at 3:00 PM. You can hear it clicking away at a speed that doesn't seem fast enough. The torture of watching as team members time their runners just makes it feel all that much slower. It's the middle of the night now, and the clock hits the twelve-hour mark. I grab the bullhorn and announce loudly from the exchange zone, "We're halfway done!" A cheer rises, but the celebration quickly dies as they realize they will double their miles before the day is over. The first half was easy. Now that the adrenaline has worn off, everyone has to rely on passion.

Passion

The final characteristic of success is **passion**. Can the passion keep them going when everything else is demanding they stop? People want success, but, too often, they don't want to work for it. Success is not achieved overnight, and it may take a lifetime. If we don't have the passion to keep going and do the little steps to keep on track, it's amazing how fast we can be on a different path. And, it's hard to get back on track. Distractions abound—so many reasons why we stop going to the gym, give up on the diet, don't pursue a career or follow through with a dream. The trick is to somehow keep going and keep moving forward. Even if it's slow, small steps, when we look back, we will be surprised at how far we've come and how many people we've lapped. Passion is the key. The second half of the event is when the runners need that passion to keep going without walking. One mile at a time, one lap at a time, or break it down to every curve and straight away on the track, and keep going. Before they know it, they are one more mile and one step closer to finishing. Fighting through the cold or light rain, aching muscles, sore feet, exhaustion, and lack of sleep, these runners still will not walk. They know anyone can walk this event, that's not what this is about. They have trained for six weeks; some have trained all year. It's not **what** they are doing or **how** they are doing it, but **why** that keeps them going. Mentally, they are prepared to finish this tough time, knowing that if they can just keep going they will achieved **success**. They are motivated. They have passion.

My father was a Navy SEAL. If asked what sets the SEALs apart from everyone else, his answer is, "They are highly motivated." Again, it is the **why** principal. One of the many things I remember my dad mentioning was "Hell Week" and the lack of sleep the SEALs had to endure. Interestingly, he mentioned that food will substitute for sleep, at least for a period of time. With only about four hours of sleep during the entire Hell Week, food was one of the only refuges that kept him and his team awake. It's a great energizer and motivator. Now we are not doing anything close to what the SEALs do, but the lack of sleep does catch up to everyone. I experience it during the thirty six hours I'm up, and the runners feel it also. It is one of the discomforts that the runners and parents go through during this event. They learn how to endure and continue, and food plays a huge part. If they are lucky, they won't have to deal with bad weather. Food will not help with the weather, only preparation.

Everything's Wet

It's one thing to be in the cold and/or a light rain for ten minutes but it's totally different for six hours. This is a learning experience, and students learn to prepare for just about anything. In general they do a great job. Most have never experienced any discomfort from the weather because we live in a climate controlled environment. It's one aspect of making the event run as smoothly as possible that can't be controlled. During the 24 hours, odds are everyone will have to deal with adverse weather conditions. It's a great opportunity for students to see they can overcome this discomfort and how important it is to be prepared. Blankets come out to create a barrier from the cold. Sitting and waiting for their turn on the cold metal bleachers does not help keep them warm. They know they are all in the same boat, and they just have to deal with it. Running wrapped in blankets is common during the early cold chill of the night. The runners do not want to give up that last bit of warmth. After their run, students record their time, get the next runner, then make a beeline to their tent and bury themselves in anything they can to get comfortable.

Discomfort can make the hours pass very slowly. The ability to stay warm is easiest to overcome if they are prepared. The heat is the next hardest, but staying in the shade of tents, drinking plenty of water, and reducing extracurricular activities helps.

I dread the rain. It can make the event brutal for anyone. The plan is to continue running outside unless lightning or severe storms appear. Only then do we bring everyone inside to run in the gyms. That is a last resort. It presents its own set of problems. There have been a few years when we have succeeded in staying outside in the rain. The umbrellas come out, the students go into their tents, and we hunker down working with wet bleacher seats, shoes, and soggy grass. It's just another problem we hope to learn from in the long run. The first time it happened, nearly all the teams stopwatches got wet and stopped working. Not good. Timing was an integral part of the event; the runners were not just keeping track of how many miles they ran but how fast they were running. Although we had a few extra stopwatches and donated watches, we had to fix the problem and fast. Thankfully, the hand dryers in the washrooms did the task. We quickly dried the timers and we were back on track in no time. Our worst year of rain included six hours of running inside at night in a severe thunderstorm. Running thirteen laps between two gyms and two flights of stairs is not the ideal setup, but it's what we had. Providing a separate place for a couple hundred boys and girls to sleep was also a challenge. The participants rolled with the change and went right into action within minutes of the signal to clear the track. They were prepped prior to the event to help make for a smooth transition if needed. It was a disaster drill that worked the very first time. The disaster we were unprepared for was the scene of the track when we went back out after the all clear was given. The drainage system was overloaded and the infield was flooded. The north end of the infield had 2 to 3 inches of water and the tents had indoor swimming pools. Almost everyone's belongings were soaked. If that wasn't enough, several tents were not staked down well enough, and the high winds uprooted them and sent them across the open field like tumbleweeds. Tent city had taken its first major hit. Knowing we could do nothing, the runners dealt with the setback, pulled together, and waited for a positive sign. Sunrise.

PAIGE

In 6th grade, I thought to myself, "Never in a million years." Then I ran the 24 Hour Run in 7th and 8th grade. The experiences were unforgettable!

If you're tired of starting over, stop giving up! —**Unknown**

Concentrate

The sun has been hidden beyond the horizon for over seven hours, we are nearing the end of the toughest part of the entire experience, but not out of the woods yet. Fatigue has set in, the runners are physically and emotionally exhausted, sore, and cold. At this point the students keep their blankets on while on deck and during their mile run. This is often a make or break moment. Passion is tested now unlike any other time during this experience. Everybody asks, "Has anyone dropped out yet?" They want to know if the entire group will make it to the finish. No one wants to be the first or only one to not make it. The pressure is within themselves to be there for the entire group and their team. They have come this far, starting over next year is not an option for many, they realize they cannot give up.

Sometimes the best intentions are interrupted by the inability to concentrate. Everything becomes a blur, and a zombie state of mind and body surfaces. Counting to four can be difficult. Four laps on the track, that's it, but when the mind wanders and the runners are exhausted, three laps feels like four. This happens to plenty of runners during this time, that's why the timers must help keep count of the number of laps. It is tough to come sprinting into the exchange zone, thinking you're done with your mile, only to hear your timer say, "That's only three, you have one more." This sucks any remaining energy right out of them. But they keep on going.

Phone Home

This is when many of the students "hit the wall" and rely on their phones to call for help. When youngster don't feel well, the temptation to instantly communicate can spread like a disease. We understand the overpowering urge to call Mom before talking to us but the reality is, it can make the situation worse. Students need to learn to overcome the tough parts and stay on track to finish. In many cases, we want the parents to take a step back. "Are you okay? Are you hurting? Do you need me to come pick you up?" are conversations we don't want the children and their parents to have. It is too easy for runners, in a fragile state of mind, to accept the open arms of their parents and melt into their emotional and physical comfort and protection. We want to sidetrack these youngsters if possible—talk them through it, make sure they are okay, come up with a plan, and help them follow through. Students tend to respond better to us when it comes to the big picture. Having worked through the program with thousands of students, we have some techniques to help them maintain. We have a

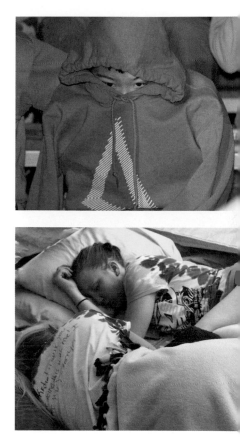

success rate of 99.93% of our students making it to the end, so we want to see if we can help first. This topic is addressed with the parents a few days before the event. Parents understand what the runners can reap from of this experience. However, when your own child is struggling or crying, the parental instinct is tough to overcome. For some parents, it's a gut-wrenching experience. I've had to console moms who were crying uncontrollably. They are torn between helping their child and trying to stay away. Sleeping in the car and watching from across the field is a growth and learning experience for Mom as well as the child. They can both came through the experience smiling and stronger than they started. This intervention has networked through the parents to a point. Parents help support each other as they step back from the process and let us intervene. It's good to hear parents tell other parents, "Let them do their job. They are really good at helping the kids. They care about them and will guide them through."

First Light

One resource we have on our side to help motivate the runners and refresh them at this point in the run is the power of the sun. Excitement is generating as the runners, sitting at the exchange zone facing east, begin to see the break of day in the treeline across the horizon. Is it the light of the rising sun or our imagination? Soon we realize it's getting brighter. The slight warmth of the new sun and knowing the night has passed is a great motivator. The last sign of the passing night comes when the diesel-powered tower lights are turned off. After seven or eight hours, we are accustomed to hearing the constant vibrating hum of the engines. The silence created when they are turned off feels refreshing! The last bit of night is erased with a flick of a switch. Quiet is all around.

ANNA

I woke my friend up to tell her she was on deck. She yelled, "No, I'm not!" and went back to sleep.

At night, I can't sleep. In the morning, I can't wake up. —**Unknown**

Sleepwalking

My overall favorite time of the day, other than the end, is this. The area is quiet, people are moving like slow, stumbling zombies and usually a light fog or mist rests on the dark grass. Parents drink coffee and everyone's eyes are a little glazed over. Rotations to the on-deck positions are moving slowly. Some of the runners are not waking up in time, even with their phone alarms set. Sleep finally overcomes many of the runners, and it hits them hard. This is the most difficult time to wake the runners. They are in a deep sleep. Calling their name outside the tent doesn't work. We have to physically shake them awake. They tend to be in a sleepwalking cycle, unable to comprehend it is their turn on deck. A video of their reactions would be highly entertaining—expressions and reactions are funny to watch. One of three results usually happens when they are awakened. Some spring up with a quick, "Yea, okay," throw on their shoes, and head out. The other two reactions are a little more interesting. Some refuse to wake up. After an earthquake of shaking, they grumble some inaudible sound, then silence. We hit them with another tremor, and they slowly rise. Now most would think they are up and alert enough to exit the tent and show up to their post; however, it doesn't happen that way. We can't leave their side or they will collapse right back into a deep sleep. Standing at the door, we keep encouraging them to find their shoes and leave the comfort of the tent. Once they actually leave the tent, the pieces usually connect, and they find their way to their post. The most

amusing ones are those who get up but are not awake. They look at us wide-eyed and tell us they just ran, then flop back into their blankets. With another quick nudge, they pop up as if it is the first time we are attempting to wake them. This time, they agree they need to get up but they just sit up and don't move. They just stare at us and keep saying, "Yea." We try not to laugh and ask them to put on their shoes. It would seem this is the most complicated maneuver they have ever performed. Anything goes now: not putting on shoes, being unable to find shoes, putting on two different shoes or wrong shoes, and/or putting shoes on the wrong feet. I have even had kids fight to get their foot into a shoe that is facing backwards and not understand why it is not working. Finally it's figure out. Regardless of how the shoes go on, they try to either go back to bed or walk to their post. After a minute or two on deck, they don't even remember what transpired, but now, they are awake.

Stomach Aches

Sometimes getting runners up is the easy part. Once, we had a dozen participants curled up in the tents, crying because their stomachs hurt. We had an epidemic and didn't know the source of the problem. After asking questions, we figured it out. It was the year energy and power drinks grew popular. These youngsters had tried to stay

up all night by drinking this liquid and filling up on bread donated by a restaurant. Trying to stop the hemorrhaging, we got everyone better liquids and more substantial food. In about a half hour, the problem was solved. Energy drinks are now strictly forbidden and more attention is given to educating runners on proper food and drink choices before and during the event. Nutrition plays a much bigger role in the student's preparations. Conditioning alone is not enough. Making healthy choices for this challenge—fruits, good sandwiches, proper snacks, and water—along with eating smaller amounts more often contributes to their success in finishing.

A Time to Shine

The preparation and ability to complete the event is possible for any student who remains focused on everything we tell them. What about the introverted, quiet kids who struggle to focus in class and generally seem lost in the school setting? Some have factors that make it difficult to perform at an average or above average level. Every year, we have one or two of these students sign up. Do they have the ability to follow the strict guidelines and handle the responsibility required to be successful in this program? With hesitation, and with hope, we wait and see. Interestingly, they often become the most focused, on time, responsibility-driven, and helpful participants in the event. This happens repeatedly. It's as if this is what they needed in life—a chance to prove themselves. There is something about the 24 Hour Run these students latch onto, something that transcends daily learning in the school environment. Here they shine. I have not isolated what it is, or why, but for them it works. These students rarely say anything in or out of class, but we see it in their faces. They love this! They look forward to it all year. When these students sign up, I'm not worried. I smile. I cannot wait to see them rise above the challenges.

GRACE

My favorite memory was sitting at my tent eating cold noodles and watching the sunrise.

79

I already want to take a nap tomorrow! —**Unknown**

Sleep Deprivation

Sleep deprivation is an interesting experience, and the biggest challenge for me to overcome. By 6:00 AM, I have been up for 26+ hours, without rest, and on my feet for approximately 15 miles. I still have at least 10 hours and 5 to 8 miles of being on my feet before I go home. I strongly believe everyone should go through this experience and know what this feels like to be up working for that long. We come to appreciate what our body can do and the sacrifices others have made. Hell Week for my dad in Navy SEAL training must have been excruciating. My 36 hours is nothing compared to his week of nearly no sleep. It's an interesting experience because of how it plays with our senses. As long as we have something that keeps us moving and focused, we tend to be alright, just tired. When we sit or have nothing to keep us occupied everything changes. Sounds become unclear and disorient-

ing, movement is hard to track, and our physical capabilities are slow and clumsy. The ability to focus and process information is drastically reduced, the brain needs to conserve energy. My attention span becomes that of a goldfish, and my ability to process information is running on empty. I struggle to remember where I'm walking to on the field. Speech becomes a struggle as I try to find the words to finish some of my thoughts. None of this feels particularly good, but I enjoy the challenge, and the parents and kids seem to enjoy watching me struggle to stay awake. To get off my feet

for a few minutes, I usually put a chair in the exchange zone facing the runners. As I mentioned before, sitting does not help matters—my eyelids stop working and are nearly impossible to hold open. I can feel my head bobbing as I struggle to open my eyes and gaze around as if it was one fluid intentional movement. After about 30 seconds, the struggle becomes too great. I go into a lucid dream state. I see visions or dreams, but can still hear what's going on around me. My brain tries to make sense of it all and eventually some loud noise or laughter snaps me back into reality. The laughing is usually because someone has just taken a photo of me in my temporary state of suspended animation. I'm just glad nobody was around when I fell asleep on the toilet one year! Once, I gave into the power of sleep in about five seconds. I sat down to talk with a coworker and woke up to him laughing hysterically. I had just fallen asleep in mid-sentence. I didn't even get a full sentence out before sleep overpowered me, my words slowly drifting away into silence. I convinced myself I just needed some food and sunlight, and I could make it through the rest of the day. The runners get to take advantage of something more to wake them up, something that's only available once a year at Lundahl. The showers!

Hit the Showers

Showers in our district, and in many schools, are no longer used in physical education or athletics due to the invasion of personal privacy. The shower rooms are now used as storage areas. Without getting into health or social issues about this, I'm not sure this is a step in the right direction. We bring up the topic of using the showers in our meetings, and we let the students know they will be open for about two hours. They usually think we are kidding or that we are a little strange for even bringing up this topic. The reality is that this will be the best shower they have ever taken. They will feel 100% better afterwards. We really encourage them to take advantage of this opportunity—bring swimsuits, boxers, or whatever makes them comfortable. They won't regret this water break. We still don't get many that take advantage of this, but the ones who do are like little kids again, playing in sprinkler. I sit in my office (out of sight of the showers) to make sure nothing goes wrong and check emails. There is constant yelling and laughing, and the students take forever. Slowly they emerge from the steam filled room saying exactly what we told them: "That was awesome!" "That was the best shower ever!" They are revitalized. Throwing on clean underwear and socks completes the transformation. These runners are ready to finish the challenge with new-found energy.

LAUREN

A funny memory was when my friend was being awakened by a parent volunteer, and she wasn't quite awake. When asked to get out of the tent, she replied, "Why? Why do I have to run outside? Where am I?" I then had to help her get her shoes on and escort her out of the tent. While she was walking with the parent to the bleachers we could hear her talking, still confused.

*It's very easy to be different, but it's very
difficult to be better.* —**Jonathon Ive**

They Are Still Running

Our first year, around 7:00 AM, the teachers arrived at school and were shocked: "They were serious. I can't believe they're still running!" I overheard this comment as I entered the school office. I went about my business, but now colleagues were interested in what had transpired during the night and how the students were doing. I answered questions with an exhausted smile and what energy I had left. The student runners and the event were the main topic of conversation for the rest of the day. A total flip of emotion occurred in much of the staff. They were impressed and in awe of what these students were doing. The school climate was changing, and we began getting the support we were hoping for: "This is the best morale booster the school has ever had for teachers and students." "This is the best thing I've ever seen happen at this school."

About this time every year, students arriving for Friday classes gather at the edge of the track talking to the runners: "How you doing?" "How hard is it?" "How many miles have you completed?" "Have you slept at all?" This is when runners who were "on the fence" about participating or dropped out of the program earlier decide to take part next year and make it through. They see the achievement and excitement on the faces of their fellow students. They want the same experi-

ence. When we raise the bar, people rise up and take the challenge. During the day, teachers bring their classes out to support the runners. By the end of the day, for the last hour, nearly the entire school is at the edge of the track with banners, cheering their friends on. The runners are like celebrities. It is awesome to see the excitement of people on both sides of the track.

I knew this event wasn't just something different. I knew the experiences the runners received could make them better students and athletes. Sometime during the 24 hours, they experience something like never before and learn something about themselves along the way. Those experiences have to be learned by doing instead of discussing or reading about. "Experiential education" is a great learning tool. Whether it's a program or an individual, being different is not always better, being different is easy. Doing something better is what makes the event worthwhile. That is what I want this 24 Hour Run to be. Not just different, but better than anything else they experience. As I felt the climate and the energy of the school change that first year, I knew that we had accomplished something not just better, but extraordinary.

RYAN

My favorite part was playing board games while waiting.

It doesn't matter what others are doing.
It matters what you are doing. —**Sarsuki Shibuya**

Food Is Awesome

Tired and worn out in the morning, food is a great pick-me-up and can help a lot of problems fade away. The body is craving the nutrients it depleted. Whether it is mental or physiological, we crave the foods for which our bodies are starving. Food tastes awesome! Certain foods just taste great when camping out in the fresh air, and most people seem to have a comfort food. Campers even find themselves eating food they wouldn't normally eat at home. Cold, bruised, mushy, or slightly damp, it doesn't seem to matter—food is a welcome reward.

About this time, the teachers are in their classrooms, and student spectators hurry to class. The track is once again left to the runners who have been pounding their feet over 1,600 times for every mile they accomplish. The energy boost just received is quickly fading. Still wrapped in blankets, their faces show exhaustion and they slowly return to auto pilot. They are back to focusing on their tasks. As the morning sun warms them, their personalities return from the cold of the night. I ask if they are having fun, and, no matter how tired or cold they are, the answer is always, "Yes!"

Head Lice

When don't they have fun? Finding out they have head lice! Early one morning, a mom came to me and said, "My daughter's tent partner has lice." I was not expecting this to ever happen. We ask students to pack their tents with friends during the event. If it's a six person tent, we want six to eight people using the tent. Since all the runners are not in the tent at the same time, there should be room, and it's easier to find them. But if one person has lice, then everyone in the tent has to be checked. We kept the news quiet to avoid a panic. All the girls headed up to the school nurse to be checked. The only one infected was the carrier, luckily everyone else was cleared. The rule is that a student with lice cannot be at school. We called the parents to pick her up. It's not the way anyone wants to go home. I don't think that group of girls spent any more time inside that tent's nylon walls.

🏃 MACKENZIE

I've been waiting to do the 24 Hour Run since 3rd grade when I saw my sister do this. I can't believe I'm now doing this three years later and trying to beat my sister's miles.

All things are difficult before they are easy. —**Thomas Fuller**

We Have a Visitor

The most difficult time has passed, everyone is gearing up for the last remaining hours. The rest is easy. At least in theory. The event still has a way to go, but we can see a light at the end of the tunnel. Students know they can make it from here. Everyone is still in zombie-mode as they time their runner. But a new spark comes. Sometimes an unexpected source of fuel jump-starts the runners.

Two years in a row, participants got the boost they were looking for—though not by choice. Unbelievably, we had two different adults visit the track on two back-to-back years. This is a closed course, no one is allowed in unless part of the event. It was evident these two were not with our group. Both men were prob-

ably in their early thirties, and neither one was functioning to their full capacity. Either they had some disabilities or were still partying from the night before. The first year this happened the man was "right out of the 60s." He was barefoot, dressed in tie-dye clothing, with a knit hat and dreadlocks. He was pointed out to me on the track. I approached him, asked if I could help, and received no response. I told him he could not be there and that he needed to leave. By this time, we had walked side-by-side halfway around the track and were now on the straight away to the exchange zone. Students had been running past us the entire time as if we were in the slow lane of traffic. I needed to get him to leave somehow, but he wasn't responding. Suddenly, everything changed. He

yelled out, "I want to run!" He took off running toward the exchange zone, shoulder checking runners and running through them. In a split second, I think to myself that I've been up for 29 hours, I'm exhausted, my legs and feet hurt, and now I have to go catch this guy. I took off in a full sprint. I felt like I was in a dream with my feet stuck in mud, and I needed to use my hands to claw the ground to get more speed. I could hear students and parents yelling from the sidelines as he clipped each of the runners. After fifty yards, I caught up to him at the exchange zone. Still running, I hooked him under his armpit with my arm and forced him to run off the track. I used my "coaching voice" and demanded that he leave the premises immediately. Other parents were involved as he actually tried to get back onto the track. Barricading the track with our bodies, we told him to leave. He tried to out-dodge us one or two more times then slowly walked away. My adrenaline pumping, I watched him walk out of sight. The students were all okay. They were all wide awake! I tried to downplay the whole situation and not draw attention. Rumors flew and, within minutes, everyone heard about the incident, but their version was a little different. According to the rumors, I tackled the guy and threw him off the track. I quickly tried to defuse the story. The runners were so excited, even some of the parents were pumped. Later we laughed about the whole experience—it is one I won't forget.

The next year, I couldn't believe we had another visitor, even at the same time. I thought, "You have to be kidding me!" This time someone different was walking the track and a little unstable. There was no way the same event was going to occur again this year. I immediately blocked his path and demanded he leave. Once again, no feedback, and he tried to stay on the track. This year though, the parents who had seen the incident the previous year also stepped into action. They helped block his path and convince him this was not the place for him to be. With several adults in his way, he decided to back down and walk a different path. Although he hung around in the distance for a little while, he eventually left the area, this time with no confrontation and no rumors. We were able to keep the peace and keep activities running smoothly.

50 Miles

Students also keep the peace by staying in the proper rotation! The plan is for the runners to be present and ready to run in their rotation and all will run smoothly. This way, the rest of the team gets the break they need. If runners are interested in pushing themselves to run extra miles, that's fine, as long as they do not exhaust themselves. They need to be able to take their next turn in the rotation when it comes. Students usually do a great job at this. But some students want to do more miles than they can attain in their team rotation. One year, we heard a rumor that someone was going for a record. Luke and Nina were siblings and great runners. They were excited about running and willing to train any chance they got. So much so, that when they got grounded at home and sent to

their rooms, they climbed out the window and went for a run. They definitely had passion. The problem was Luke was not taking breaks between runs, or only very short ones. In the middle of the night, he had already completed a marathon and showed no signs of letting up. We kept an eye on him. We wanted to make sure he was alright and

actually completing his miles. He was. We asked him to slow down and save some energy, but he just kept going. It was early morning when we felt we had to make a safety call. Even after we told him to stop he continued to sneak onto the track to get in another mile. I physically had to hold him by the shoulders and tell him not to run anymore. By that time, he had already run 50 miles! We had to make a decision on what this event was about and take his safety into consideration. I was sure he could run another 20 miles but this was also a team effort. Luke made his point. He loved to run and he was good at it. He will go down as running the most miles ever in the 24 Hour Run. After that year, we were forced to put a limit to the number of miles a participant could complete. That number equals a marathon, 26.2 miles! The stipulation that accompanies this new rule is that runners have to pace themselves so they finish around 3:00 PM. We have a good system in place to help make that happen. We can help anyone who wants to go for the goal to be with their team when it's their turn to run, all the way through the finish. The marathon is now a goal at least 20 to 30 people attempt each year.

Follow the Rules

We had never kicked anyone out for running too much or testing the rules and integrity of the event, until Maggie came along. This was probably the hardest decision we ever had to make during the event. Maggie was a 7th grader, one of the top athletes in school, and a good person; however, she had a slightly arrogant attitude. The rules didn't always apply to Maggie, from her perspective. This was the scene in our regular physical education classes and in the sports she played. The other students were aware of this. Every year we talk to the runners about the 26.2 mile limit and why it is in place. Runners are told that if they finish early, it puts a hardship on their team. The consequence of finishing early is being sent back to class to finish the school day on Friday. We thought that rule and warning would be enough. Not for Maggie. We found out early Friday that she had completed her marathon and was no longer running. When I caught up with Maggie, her mom was also present. It didn't take long for the conversation to get heated. Keeping the situation under control was not easy. We let her know that, according to the rules, she now had to go to class for the rest of the school day. She had just spent 18 hours camping and running. It seemed like a death sentence to send her back to school and banish her from the track. Questions and rumors flew from both sides of the track, but we had no choice. We had to follow through or our integrity and the program's integrity would not have the same value. Maggie put up a fight but reluctantly went back into the building. I escorted her to class. No one could believe what they were seeing. Everyone was astonished to see us enter the classroom. I felt as if I had just walked her into a prison cell and shut the door, leaving her with the other inmates. Her mom and the principal were supportive of the decision, but it was not an easy choice even though I felt it was the right one. Maggie did not make eye contact with me the rest of the day, until the end. Still unhappy and feeling she was treated unfairly, I asked her to join us for our final lap at the conclusion of the event and the closing speech. I am sure it was not easy for Maggie to come back and face everyone at the

end, but she was strong and determined.

Nearly a year passed before I saw Maggie in the crowd at our first meeting for the next 24 Hour Run event. I was surprised. After the prior year's incident, I figured she hated the 24 Hour Run, or at least me. When I discussed the rule about finishing early with the students, I could feel everyone looking at Maggie. Everyone knew what I was talking about. Maggie kept a low profile. I caught up with her during the run on one of her breaks. She brought up how she felt and that she had not planned on participating. The problem was, she got excited and wrapped up in the hype that the run was coming. Up until the incident last year, she had a great time participating. She decided to give it one more try and was committed to doing everything right. That word "no" made her stronger and more driven. It's one of those experiences every successful person needs to explore. She admitted she had matured and that she was cocky the previous year. Maggie also said that "it sucked," but she learned from the experience and was better because of it. This Maggie was not the same person I knew a year ago! She had become a young adult, not the girl that always got her way. The talk was short but good, and I'm glad we had the chance to clear the air. I am very proud of her and her decision to come back and do it again. Maggie did wonderfully that second year. I have no doubt that success will continue to be part of her future! Her story is now legend among the runners. Since then, no one has finished the run early.

ANONYMOUS

My favorite memory was at around 3 AM I was really tired and had convinced myself I couldn't run anymore but my friend convinced me I could and I got my best mile time.

Character is what you do when you don't think
others are watching —**John Wooden**

You're Doing Great

As I make my rounds and observe the students, I ask if they are doing okay and acknowledge their responses. I give the students running on the track all the motivation I can and let them know they are doing awesome as they pass by. They continue as if I am not there or they don't hear me—they are focused. The reality is, I know they hear my comments. I know this for two reasons. The students write about the 24 Hour Run in some of their assignments, and that little motivation as they pass, is one of the moments they remember that kept them going. It can be the little things we do as teachers, they sometimes remember most. The other reason is, I heard it first hand when I ran the event.

When people asked if I was running, my comment was, "I'm running the event, I don't have time to actually run." It was a little bit of a cop out, but some truth was in it. I couldn't do both, at least that's what I kept telling myself. My daughter Corryn had gone through the program for three years, my son was doing it for the second time in 7th grade. I started feeling guilty about asking all these students and my own children to challenge themselves when I had not even given it a try. Demonstrating what I taught was something I felt strongly about as a teacher. If I was ever going to run, now was the time—with my son, Ben. My colleague Susie Johannesen had been asking for more responsibility with the event. We

worked out the details, and I had no reason not to run. I was actually a little nervous. What if I couldn't finish? I would never hear the end of it. I had to make a commitment. I decided to train in the same way I asked the students to train. I realized I was not a particularly good runner and more out of shape than I thought. I only hoped I could get it all together. I decided I wanted the full experience and that running a marathon was the challenge I needed. On the day of the event, I was as excited and as nervous as the students. The starting gun exploded, and I felt good my first few miles. While running in the event, I experienced something I had not realized was going on, something I had not heard before, or at least noticed. The amount of encouragement was awesome, not just when finishing the run, but as people passed or as I passed them while running. There was constant encouragement: "Good job!" "You're doing great!" This wasn't just toward me, but everyone on the track. It provided a little boost of energy every time someone noticed me and said words of encouragement. At around 18 miles, my knees felt like they had sand in them. Every step was a killer. I knew that if I stopped I might never have another chance to do this. I had to push on. When I was passed by the students and given words of encouragement, I knew I was not alone out there. I had a support group running with me. I finished my marathon without walking, as was expected, and had an experience that was powerful. Encouragement was one of those hidden positive aspects of the event that showed what kind of students were involved. They had character. It showed. This was not a competition, but a group effort. We were all in this together.

 ALEXUS

The 24 Hour Run has showed me that hard work pays off. I wanted to show my dad and brother I could do it and show how strong I am. On the Thursday we started the run, my grandma passed away that morning. So I did this for her. I am also doing the color run 5K in June this summer.

Don't let school get in the way of your education. —**Mark Twain**

Reflections

Our students learn more about themselves during these 24 hours, than many learn in a lifetime. This is also true of the parents. The experiences (emotional, physical, and/or social) are stripped of superficial layers, raw. **This is experiential education in its truest form.** We think we know what to do in a given situation but, until we live it, we don't really know. We spend a lot of time in school teaching great ideas, pouring over information, preparing students for tests, doing research, but not always actually performing. These experiences of the 24 Hour Run provide opportunities for failure and success and chances to really see possibilities and potential. These moments also provide for additional learned skills that are equally important but subtle. These experiences fill the gaps and connect the things students have learned. Our bodies and brains can process these experiences much easier, enabling them to recall the lessons more clearly for a longer period of time. The trick is to make sure participants understand the miles they run are the **what** in the equation. The **why** is what the students are capable of—setting goals and applying the characteristics of success. Then they can apply this experience to life in a more efficient, proven manner, with confidence. Cooking, fixing a bike, building something, caring about someone, and so many other experiences in our lives give us pride in what we have accomplished and the confidence to keep moving forward.

I've had countless conversations with parents and students on how this experience changed their attitude, behavior, and for some, their lives. It is these heart-to-heart conversations during and after the event that help runners connect what they learn here to life. This connection may occur when they experience uncertainty or lack of confidence during the event, in the classroom, or in another life situation. We let them know we have confidence in them and remind them to draw upon and continue to apply the skills we learned (characteristics of success). By sharing in their successes and letting them know we're proud of them, we encourage them to reapply their success and skills to other parts of their lives. Some of these stories and lessons are then highlighted in the closing speech and debriefing at the end of the event.

By this time of the day, participants are feeling good about themselves. They know they can make it to the end. They share stories with each other about the fun times, miles accomplished, the food eaten, and how much they have slept. The runners tell me how awesome this is or that this is the best day ever. They experience so much and get a taste of success. They cannot help but feel great. Success achieved through hard work is a rare feeling we don't get from anything else. These students are achieving goals they did not think were possible six weeks ago.

RYAN

I couldn't find my shoes so I had to run in my boots. It was cold and I ran holding an orange and kept sucking on it the whole way.

Knowledge does not equal understanding. —**Destin Sandlin**

Will I Make My Goal?

We do not understand a skill until we accomplish the skill. Until then we only have knowledge. There is a difference. Students think, along with most adults, that they understand this concept but they don't. I can provide the information—knowledge—required to ride a bike; however, until the students can actually ride, they won't have understanding of how to ride a bike. This is why hands-on experience is key for education. People must understand in order to learn. After the 24 Hour Run experience, students are able to take what they learn and apply it in different areas of their life and build on that.

Setting the goal is knowledge, achieving the goal is understanding! Runners have set goals in this event for years, and most achieve their goals. Many achieve it earlier in the event by beating their fastest times or becoming a team leader. Others have to wait until the finish to realize if they made their goal of "X" amount of miles run or prove to others they can do this. Their goal is that little bit of incentive to stay on track, and it is also a way to better understand their own capabilities.

What if I set a goal for everyone, would they achieve that also? In our eighth year, I did just that. The program continued to grow, with more students, more miles, and more success stories. After adding up the miles from previous years, I realized we were close to going around the world, about 25,000 miles. I thought it would be great to finish that goal by the end of the event that year. This was not going to be easy, we would need more runners and more miles than in any other year. Finishing the distance at the end of this year would, however, be more powerful than getting it done in the first several hours of the following year. This was the year to make that goal. With our first week of training, we had more than enough participants to get the miles required, as long as everyone survived the training and then the event. As the weeks rolled by, we started dropping in numbers, it would be close if I had done the averages correctly. I originally asked everyone to put in one extra mile outside of their rotation to get the required distance. Everyone was fine with that and pumped this would be the year. With 389 runners, it was our biggest year so far by over 50 participants. Forty percent of the school was participating! On the day of the event I redid the math. Because the number of runners had dropped from our first week, the total result of everyone doing one more mile would not reach the goal.

A half-hour before we started, I had to break the news. My stomach was in knots, I felt I was letting everyone down, but I had to be honest. Instead of disappointing them, I went in asking them for more. I wanted every single person to give me their best, not by adding one mile, but by adding four! They had to average sixteen miles each. The students were stunned. The gym was silent as I explained the situation. I told them they were capable, this would be a tough 24 hours, and we were counting on each person to do his/her part. Everyone wanted to get this goal this year. Adding the extra miles was going to be tough. They accepted the challenge. Students were excited as they completed their miles, letting me know the extra ones they accomplished. They were proud to contribute to the goal. I couldn't believe the size of the group that year and the extra miles they were doing. At 3:00 AM, we

did a count to see if we had half our goal. We were close, really close. As the hours ticked down, the miles added up. The question was, "Are we going to make it around the world this year?" Parents and myself kept adding the miles, nervously, wondering if we would have enough. It was not until the last hour that I knew for sure. We made our goal! I held the information until the final speech at the close of the event. I wanted to tell everyone at once. When the announcement was made, the crowd cheered as if we had just made the winning touchdown in the Super Bowl.

I am always proud of my students as they do this event, but the year of making the round-the-world goal was something a little extra. They went above and beyond what was expected in the event. I asked them to, and they gave me everything they had with enthusiasm.

NATALIE

Me and my best friend Samantha found a huge spider in my tent and we sadly got too scared, so we slept outside.

1:00 PM

Today I do what others won't, so that tomorrow
I can accomplish what others can't. —**Jerry Rice**

Success Is Within Reach

There are only two hours left, and runners know they only have one or two miles left to run. They cannot believe it is almost over. They just spent the last 22 hours with several hundred others on the infield of the track, running mile relays to see if they have what it takes. In two hours, they will know for sure, but the odds at this point are good. Everyone is running on energy reserves, struggling to remain focused for their last remaining duties. Parents are rolling in to support their athletes in these final hours. It feels different than the start of the event. A "feel good" energy is in the air, without the chaos. Everyone started with individual goals and expectations, however, it feels more like a community or family in these final hours. Parents share stories with each other about their child's experience as well as their own. Students have learned through experience how to pace themselves and the importance of stretching—the knowledge that training makes a difference is clear. They have learned how to plan, predict, and pack for 24 hours and the value of watching weather reports. This event provides them with a chance to look deep inside themselves to see what motivates them. They learn to help motivate others and realize others count on them. Some learn to maintain a fire and realize they don't have to look their best to have fun. Just sitting around the tent or fire with friends is good. By doing this, they make new friendships and strengthen old ones. They learn that one hour of sleep only feels like two minutes when someone wakes them up to run. They discover food tastes great in fresh air, and hot showers are fantastic.

The runners have proven to be more responsible and independent in one day than others will all year. During this whole process, they can learn as much, or more, from their failures as their successes. They realize they can keep going when they think they can't. They learn confidence, respect, and pride for themselves when overcoming difficult obstacles. They know how to take an overwhelming obstacle, break it down into smaller chunks, and make their goal possible. They have done something that most others don't have a chance to experience. Along the way, they learned lessons that will allow them to accomplish more in their life.

 ANONYMOUS

It was fun, laughing and giggling in my tent with all my friends.

*Experience is what you get when you don't get
what you wanted.* —**Randy Pausch**

Disability or Ability

A unique aspect of the 24 Hour Run is anyone in the school can participate with no prior talent or experience. Students with a wide range of running skills, body sizes and strengths, as well as mental focus and toughness participate. Each just has to want the prize more than the desire to stop. To go beyond their comfort levels and continue is uncharted territory for some.

Kyle was a 6th grader, and running was way outside of his comfort zone. He cried every time we ran any distance on the track in our physical education class. He sobbed uncontrollably, expressing his belief that he could not possibly run all four laps, and then he shut down. Kyle came a long way over the years with us. He took on the "Warrior Training" unit in 8th grade to see how much he could challenge himself (see What's Next on page 115), and at the end of his 8th grade year, he did the 24 Hour Run. The purpose was to challenge himself one more time. He never complained, even when we did the 2½ miles, and he talked about all the running he was doing at home. It was great to see the boy become a young adult, both in his emotions and his physical abilities. Kyle was proud of his accomplishments. He took on challenges instead of backing away.

For some, it's a way to prove that a disability is nothing more than just being different and that they are as unique as everyone else. Andy was a normal middle-schooler who did all the activities most middle-school boys do, including basketball. We noticed nothing out of the ordinary about him other than a slight imbalance in his stride. I

didn't think anything unusual of it—it was just the way he walked. It was in gymnastics class that I realized why his walk was slightly different. I had asked him to demonstrate a skill on the balance beam for the class. As he performed the skill in his socks, I noticed one foot was only about half the size of the other. Andy's performance was fine, and we moved on. I asked him to stop by my office at the end of class. I was curious and wanted to ask about his foot. We had an open conversation in which he explained it was the result of a boating accident. While tubing with a family member as a child, the rope got tangled on the prop, sucked in their tube, and sliced off half his foot. Andy didn't let it bother him and only his close friends knew about his injury. It was obvious that he didn't see it as an excuse or a disability. Performing the 24 Hour Run was just one more obstacle he wanted to overcome. His injury wasn't going to slow him down. Andy completed the event without any problems, finishing a marathon. I asked him if I could mention him and his injury during the final speech about overcoming adversity. This was the first time everyone would know about his condition. Both parents and students applauded and cheered when he was introduced. At that moment, he became an inspiration to many. I hope his story encourages others to take this challenge or other challenges in their life regardless of their ability or disability.

MONET

I was born deaf and have implants to hear. But I don't let that stop me and always try my hardest. This run has given me a chance to prove that even though I have a disability, I can do what anyone else can.

Impossible—I'm possible.

The Final Lap

Everyone is watching the clock tick down the final minutes and seconds of the 24 Hour Run, but it's not over yet. The area is suddenly more crowded than ever as fellow students, entire families, and friends come to see the last few minutes of the event and the final lap. The last of the runners are on the track, and we are trying to figure out who is going to be the last runner to finish. Once we are sure who it is, I get on the bullhorn and summon all runners to the exchange zone. Students flank either side, leaving the center lanes open. As the last runner heads toward me on his/her final lap, everyone is cheering and the energy is at its peak. It's the gun lap.

The final lap is the same every year, but it was the first year that brought everyone to tears. The sight was unbelievable. By luck, the last runner was Chris, an 8th grade student. He was about to start his final lap on the final minute of the event. He ran up to me, and I handed him the school flag. Without breaking stride, he accepted. I fired the pistol to signify the final lap. Exhausted, every runner gathered up the strength for one more lap. Some could barely move. A jog seemed impossible, but they didn't quit. Chris was leading the pack at a slow pace but no one passed. He would lead everyone one final time around the track. The wave of colored shirts running as a group to finish their journey together is a fantastic sight any year, but there was a significant difference that first year. Chris was not the most popular student in school. In fact, he was probably the most picked on. He was a small, skinny, non-athletic, socially-awkward, nice, intelligent, middle-school student. To my knowledge he was never recognized for anything in school

and was very quiet. Not today. Not this time. He was not lost in the crowd. This was his time to shine, to finish his eighth-grade year, it was perfect. Parents were running across the field and along the track to get photos of the crowd and cheer everyone to the finish. His parents were on the sideline, crying, as he brought everyone in across the finish line. Other parents were caught up in the emotion of this powerful ending to an exhausting and exhilarating journey. Right then, he was the most popular. He was the leader, and was honored for it. This could not have happened to a better person, at a better time, and it set a precedent and mood for the years following.

We had taken what was considered "Impossible" by so many and changed it to "I'm/Possible!" Since then, we've made it possible for all to see what the students are capable of achieving. Each year the last lap has its own stories to tell, but that first year was incredibly special for all involved.

 **CAROLYN**

My favorite memory—The Victory Lap!

Final Speech & Debriefing

If I can change your Awareness, then I can change your Attitude.
Attitude changes Behavior, and Behavior can change your Life.
—**Tony Calabrese & Fred Kaiser**

As teachers, we all hope to experience that one defining moment when we realize we just changed the course of someone's life for the better. When that moment happens to over 100 students, and when those student and their parents and the administration all recognize the moment at the same time, it's life changing. That high point in my career was right then—the end of our first 24 Hour Run. I was overwhelmed with emotion as students sat around me at the finish with parents in the background to debrief the events that had just transpired. What I worked so hard for, when nearly everyone thought it was too tough and felt it wouldn't happen, suddenly hit me in a wave of pressure I could not contain. Against all odds we did it! This was the highlight of my young career. It was the best teaching moment I could have asked for. I struggled to gain composure, to begin talking. As I looked up and into the crowd, everyone was wiping away tears, and I hadn't even spoken yet. This was not going to be easy. By the time I finished, it seemed as though everyone was touched by the success of the event and the closing words.

This was only the first moment like this to occur at the closing of a 24 Hour Run.

The debriefing is one of the most important aspects of the event. It allows for a connection and understanding about why we do this event. It provides reflection on one's self and closure with a vision to move forward. This is a chance for everyone to understand that running was not the most important lesson learned. Running was the tool used to teach the lessons and skills in a way that made a connection and could be applied in this event.

Each year key points are talked about. I always recognize parents for their help and sacrifices to support their children. When asked how many students reached their goal, a sea of hands always rises. This confirms their ability and their understanding of the importance of goals—how to achieve them by breaking them down and following through. Time is spent on the four characteristics of success and how they are achieved through this event. I want them to see how these characteristics can be applied in a job, to new goals, and to other adventures. No matter the weather or the number of runners, the average mile time always lands at 8:33, give or take 5 seconds each year. I think that's impressive, considering runners times slow down during the middle of the night and the number of miles they run. I'm proud of these athletes every year, and their parents are proud of them also. I want them to understand not only what they did, but what the whole group was able to accomplish. It's up to them to take those feelings and accomplishments and apply them to other challenges. They did a great job, and they know it! On the years when no one has dropped out, it's powerful to know that everyone completed the challenge. Students often ask, "Did we make it, has anyone dropped out yet?" They always feel good when I let them know we've made it so far. I love being able to tell the group that the number of students that started 24 hours ago is the same number that finished. Runners remember if their year was one that everyone made it to the end, and they're proud of that accomplishment.

I start hours ahead of time thinking about what I want to say at the conclusion. I try to make notes if I can about some of the highlights of that year's event that make it memorable or special. With no sleep, organizing my thoughts and remembering them can be a little difficult. Often times, I can't remember the simplest of words and my public speaking is at its worst. I know what I want to say, but I can't always deliver. It doesn't seem to matter, though, as parents keep telling me they can't wait for the final speech. Apparently, it's one of those moments many parents look forward to, and in recent years, nearly every adult seems to be capturing that moment on video. The one challenge that makes it even harder to speak at times, is when I get caught up in the emotion of some of the experiences or stories. I would like to blame the lack of sleep for putting me over the edge, but students and parents also get caught up in the stories. When my daughter Corryn ran for the first time in 6th grade, I felt the same pride and support for my daughter that other parents had for their children over the years. This was different than the way I felt as a runner's teacher. This was my child doing it now. When I ran with my son Ben in 7th grade, I realized how much support all the runners were experiencing while on the track. I'm moved when former students come back and tell me how they lead their life by what they learned at this event or when parents talk about how this has changed their family. When the whole story is told,

especially when everyone is caught up in the moment, it makes the memory of the event that much more impressive and unforgettable.

The last thought I always tell the parents is to have a little fun at the expense of their children when they return home. They will still be in running mode for a while, so get the video camera out and be ready. Wait five minutes after they fall asleep—this doesn't take long—then give them a nudge, tell them it's their turn to run, and see what happens. Many parents don't have the heart to do this, but some are just as much a practical joker as I am. The stories parents share are great, and they can't stop laughing while trying to tell what their child's reactions were. For the runners and their families this will be the last of the memories until next year.

JEN

I left at 11:45 PM after watching my 6th grade daughter complete her first 4 miles. When I arrived back at the track at 6:40 AM, the sun was shining and my daughter was smiling and happy. I was extremely relieved that she did not freeze, collapse, cry, or give up. I learned that my baby has grown into a strong, wonderful, tough, young lady. Feeling so much love and pride.

Home

When the students get home, sleep is an overwhelming and welcomed force. Most are totally exhausted, while others are still pumped from the experience. Either way, their beds will never have felt so good. Families will remember and share this experience for years to come, and some will return to run as alumni.

As soon as we release the runners, they clear out as fast as possible. Parents take them to the comforts of home. In the scurry to leave and the confusion of activity, items are left behind in what looks like the remnants of a tornado. Camp chairs of all kinds seem to be the item of choice to leave behind. Apparently they just could not carry that one last item. Tent poles are left in the hurry to pack up too. I've never understood leaving a whole, partially dismantled tent behind. This happens repeatedly and no one ever claims them. Every once in a while, we have one item unclaimed at the end that breaks my heart . . . a student. As we take down the big top tent, pack up the tables and chairs,

and clean up the surrounding area, we see one of the participants in the middle of the field. They're sitting on their cooler surrounded by all their gear. The runner's parents were not able to be at the end or they couldn't get a ride home with a friend. Sometimes their ride is on the way and other times nobody can be contacted. We check on them and make sure they have a ride home and that everything is alright. Most of the time they're picked up relatively quickly, and we say our last good-byes.

🏃 ROSA

I participated in the 24 Hour Run in 6th and 8th grade. It taught me that it wasn't how fast you ran—it was about finishing. Now I run 26.2 mile marathons. I have finished 3 marathons so far!

◼ Student's Favorite Memories/Thoughts

"Running the marathon in the middle of the night and doing 2 of those miles with the shoes on the wrong feet." - Elyse

"Running while watching the sun go down and the moon come up." - Laura

"When I put up my tent with help from my grandparents and help from friends." - Grant

"The very last lap was awesome! All 3 years I was right up front with the person holding the flag. We went to the Freeze (ice cream shop) afterwards and everyone was sleep deprived." - Emilia

"I love the 24 Hour Run because I get to be with my friends and have fun and do what I love." - Hailey

"Watching people get up and run when they're super tired and don't want to." - Danny

"My good friend ran the record of 50 miles in 24 hours. After that year a 26.2 mile max was imposed. I snuck in 4 more miles to get the record runner up of 30 miles. I was breaking the rules but I loved every minute of it. Mr. Kaiser showed me to love pushing my physical limits." - Duncan

"I wanted to do something that I know I wouldn't normally do. I don't really like running, but once I started training, it was actually enjoyable. It really made me stronger and it made me realize that I can do anything if I just try and practice. I don't regret doing this run." - Noelle

"The best part of being an alumni was getting to hang out and reconnect with all my former classmates." - Paige

"I got to push my limits and bond with some friends that I wasn't always very close to." - Jake

"Eating peanut butter sandwiches and drinking orange juice outside my tent at 2 AM watching people run." - Elyse

"We used the disposable cameras since iPhones weren't popular yet. I'm extremely grateful for this because this allowed us to enjoy the event even more!" - Ashley

"Sitting down and relaxing after my final mile and eating a bag of ice." - Haley

"Crossing the finish line on the last lap." - Anonymous

"Sitting with all of my friends, laughing, telling jokes, staying up late together, and being there for each other when one person was feeling down." - Anonymous

"We have been around the school district for a long time now, and this is by far the most incredible event for my kids! (And us!)" - T. family

"Beating my mile time at 2:00 AM and running a mile at 4:00 AM with a snuggle on." - Ryan

"The alumni team cranking pop music and encouraging us to finish strong." - Nate

"The excitement in the air and the pull of the starting gun. Also the countdown to 3 AM when Mr. Kaiser jabs his finger in the air and bellows, "We're half way done!" The run changed my life with the intensity. During hardships I'd reflect on the run and say, "If you could run for 24 hours you can get through this." - Mohammed

"When the kids in school cheer me on." - Jimmy

"I fell asleep in my chair and got the worst tan line." - Anonymous

"I couldn't thing of a better way to celebrate my birthday." - Mackenzie

"When I think of my time in middle school, the first thing I think of is the 24 Hour Run." - Ryan

"Being part of the 24 Hour Run the year we ran around the earth. I always looked forward to this event at the end of the school year. Enjoyed it so much I came back and ran it as an alumni." - Trevor

"Laying in the tent with my friends and watching the shadows of people walking by." - Anonymous

"It brings together kids of different groups that might not socialize otherwise. It helps new friendships develop. And kids of any athletic ability can participate." - Anonymous

"I realized that at 2 in the morning anything tastes good, including cold French fries." - Kate

"I wanted to prove to my family that I could really commit to something. I wanted to show them that I was strong and responsible enough to do this challenge and run all 3 years. I'm almost done showing them but I still got a little time left. I know I can do it." - Anonymous

"The victory lap is the best because it means you survived the 24 Hour Challenge Run!" - Auden

"Mr. Kaiser, thanks for a mom and dad date night!" - Anonymous

What's Next?

In a world of talkers, you need to be a thinker and a doer.
—**Destin Sandlin**

That first year, before the last runner left and the area was cleaned, I was asked by my principal, "What are you going to do next?" Are you kidding me? I just wanted to go home and sleep! Interestingly people want to know what else people will do after being successful in something. They expect something more from us. Although I don't feel pressure from other people when they ask, I put pressure on myself to see what I can do. We already teach some great units. However, a new one stood out as vastly different and uniquely challenging from the rest, "Warrior Training." This was a unit Tony Calabrese created and shared at the state convention. Susie Johannesen started the program for us, and I began teaching it also, but we wanted it to grow. The students were eating it up. Designed to be a self-motivated class, students are given a list of widely different challenges. All are high intensity to see what each can achieve. Two days are spent preparing the students as to **why** we do this, and **how** they are going to be challenged. Then **what** the skills are. By that time they are hooked and can't wait to get started. This unit is one of my favorites because of the drive the students exhibit. They do it because they want to, not because we tell them to. Because it's made available and they choose their challenge for the day, it works. By the time the unit is finished, they've worked harder than in any other class. Records are broken that are unbelievable. Stu-

dents enjoy a great feeling of success even if they have some temporary setbacks. It's one of their favorite programs. We have since doubled the program and are looking for ways to incorporate its ideas and skills into all of our physical education classes on a regular basis.

Warrior Training started at the same time as our first 24 Hour Run. With the success of both, I took what my principal had asked about what's next, and decided to build on seeing what the top skill levels were in the school. The 24 Hour Run was a personal challenge within a group challenge to see if students could make it through together. I wanted to make the Fitness Challenge Marathon a race to see who could finish first and to determine the top athletes in the school. After seeing what the students could do in the 24 Hour Run and Warrior Training, I knew they could take on this new challenge. Like the 24 Hour Run, no one thought this event would ever happen, including my family and friends. Even more so because of the complexity and intensity of the challenge. This didn't phase me. I moved forward. It took 1½ years in planning and approvals before the start of the first race. The Fitness Challenge Marathon was inspired by the Eco Challenge from the late 1990s. It was modeled using the same formula. Coed teams of four 8th graders compete together for 26.2 miles, a marathon. After each student fills out a three page application, the top eleven teams are chosen and the twelfth team is luck of the draw. Each participant is also required to put in ten hours of community service before the race. The course consists of 12 miles on foot, 7.55 miles on bikes, 4.25 miles on inline skates, and 2.4 miles canoeing—not necessarily all done at the same time. Orienteering is also included, and a team-building element

is experienced during the course. The teams receive a map of the course the morning of the race and navigate throughout the community to each checkpoint. This takes them to a different school in the school district. It is truly a race that experienced adults would enjoy and find challenging. The kids, however, conquer it every year with impressive results. They receive a DVD documentary that includes interviews of their experience to prove to others what most would find impossible for middle-school students to take on. The documentary can be found on YouTube: Fitness Challenge Marathon 2014 (with more to follow).

Next, I wanted to do something in the community to get people active. After throwing some hatches with some friends, an idea was formed: Why not make this into a race. On a seven-hour trip home in a van, the race was born: "Rundezvous—Frontier Survival Race." This is a race of strength, endurance, and skill. It requires skills of the early 1880s during the days of the westward expansion. Fourteen skills on a four mile course include, hatchet throwing, archery, lassoing, and fire starting, to name a few. A radically different race from the mud runs and 5k's. This race requires more strategy and skills to complete.

I enjoy putting on this race with a great friend and fellow physical education teacher, Brian Schweitzer. He shares the same passions I do. Find out more at: RundezvousRace.com. We formed a company called Endorphin Adventures, Inc. to put on this race and other adventures. More information about what we do and the company can be found at: EndorphinAdventuresInc.com.

What's next? Inspiration comes from some of the strangest places. I'm always looking to see what other cool, interesting challenges I can develop to help people be active and enjoy seeing what they are capable of doing.

◼ Acknowledgements

This project would not have been possible without the support and guidance from my family and friends. I cannot thank my wife, Trish, enough for supporting my passions and projects and giving me the time I need to dedicate to them. I'm truly lucky to have her as a friend and as my love. I thank my children, Corryn and Ben, for listening to and trying out my ideas for teaching and activities and providing feedback. And, I thank my parents, who still support me unconditionally.

I would not be where I am, loving what I do, if I wasn't inspired by fellow teachers and people in my life. My family has played a huge role in guidance, reflection, and inspiration. My brother, Chris, and sister, Kathryn, have been a part of this journey more than they realize. Their work ethics, character, and their own passions have inspired and guided me. Chris Cavert planted the seed in my head to write a book and Jerry Shea edited my tangled thoughts. I would also like to thank the following educators (in no particular order) for inspiring me and helping me find my path and enjoy the journey of my life: Tony Calabrese, Jerry Shea, Bill Quinn, Dan Creely, Brian Schweitzer, Chris Cavert, Scott McDowell, and Susie Johannesen. Their passion, character, creativity, and positive attitude have influenced me professionally, each in their own way, on a daily basis.

About the Author

Fred Kaiser has been in education since 1989. In high school, he was told that a four year college may not be in his future. He went anyway. His cooperating teacher in college was told by the University, "He may not make it through." He was the best student teacher his cooperating teacher ever had. Mr. Kaiser just wanted to teach. He received his Bachelors of Science degree in Physical Education from Eastern

Illinois University and Masters of Science in School Administration from Northern Illinois University. He began teaching in McHenry at McHenry Middle School, then came back to his roots to teach where he went to school at Lundahl Middle School in Crystal Lake, Illinois. Over the years, Mr. Kaiser has also coached basketball and wrestling.

Fred is a recognized speaker and presenter in Illinois. He holds workshops around the country, motivating teachers and students with his creative curriculums. He has been recognized and awarded nationally through the National Association of Sports and Physical Education (NASPE) and in his community for his accomplishments and contributions. Mr. Kaiser's top awards include:

NORTHEASTERN DISTRICT – (April, 2007) Illinois Middle School Physical Education Teacher of the Year Award

STATE OF ILLINOIS – (May, 2007) Illinois Middle School Physical Education Teacher of the Year Award

MIDWEST REGION – (September, 2007) Middle School Physical Education Teacher of the Year Award

NATIONAL (NASPE)– (August, 2008) Finalist of six for National Middle School Physical Education Teacher of the Year Award

In 1986, while in college, Fred and a friend started a screen printing business, Think Ink, Inc. Screen Printing and Graphic Design. This is now a family business and produces printed tee shirts nationally. In 2012, Mr. Kaiser started a business with another friend and physical education teacher, Endorphin Adventures, Inc. The company promotes adventure and risk taking activities in the outdoors. Its flagship event is Rundezvous—Frontier Survival Race, a race that includes skills from the early 1800s of outdoor survival. The company also puts on programs and training in adventure education.

Mr. Kaiser is an accomplished woodworker with a dedicated shop for building furniture. He also enjoys spending time working on his next new idea or concept for education, home, or personal challenges. Spending time with his family and friends is something he values more and more every day.

Over a dozen schools have developed their own 24 Hour Challenge Run after seeing Mr. Kaiser's presentations or the run itself. The event has been covered on local television news seven times. Lundahl Middle School is identified in the community by this event. Over the years, university students and professors from around the state have observed the 24 Hour Run, fitness marathon, and warrior training. Contact Mr. Kaiser for more information about the 24 Hour Challenge Run and his other ideas and programs:

Fred Kaiser
PhysEdFred.com
(For additional contact information and what he's up to next.)
Think Ink, Inc. — Think-Ink.com
Endorphin Adventures, Inc. — EndorphinAdventuresInc.com

Kaiser Family: Fred, Ben, Trish & Corryn